Clim
of the Box

Climbing Out of the Box

A Path of Healing from Systemic Racism

L.J. Lumpkin

with Anne Stirling Hastings, PhD

ISBN: 9798414478591

Printed and bound in the United States.

Contents

Introduction

I was born to a Black father and a Mexican mother in California. First hand I learned about racism. I have witnessed and experienced it from White People, Black People, and Mexican People. First hand I learned about being biracial, not fitting into anyone's box. First hand I learned about growing up with Christianity and finding my own spiritual path that doesn't conform to one religion.

And I learned about the trauma reaction to being treated as a threat, as lesser than, as not belonging in the big picture.

Over years of being treated as different I walked a path toward living peacefully. It began with raging about my plight, then seeing how that anger didn't change me. I went back and forth between expressing and suppressing it. It would shoot out like a fire hose, chaotic and uncontrollable after being suppressed for so long. Finally I learned skills to actually release it.

Then I faced the fear that replaces anger. Fear when a White woman let her dogs off leash in an outdoor public gym. And how I calmed the fear with my methods. Breathing in four seconds, out eight. Leaning forward, moving energy, raising my arms over my head.

My history-loving father gave me information that helped make sense of racism. A teacher taught me yoga to calm myself. When in college I discovered how to show White friends how my life is different from theirs.

I used the accepting, supporting nature of barber shops to talk to find a sense of community. I know that most Black men will understand the culture there. The place where conversation is welcomed, where we don't have to look like a White

> *We don't have to look like a White prescription of Blackness.*

prescription of Blackness. As I became psychologically educated I offered thoughts to some of the men who were struggling with issues. And I imagined doing videos of issues common to Black men. Playing them on the TV screen in the barber shop.

I wove into this drugs, alcohol and sex to numb the pain. Playing loud music with car windows open. Getting in fights. Getting arrested.

When my psychologist writer friend and colleague Anne Stirling Hastings said that I needed to write a book on all of this for young Black men struggling with what I had been – and still am – struggling with, I liked the idea. So in weekly conversations I poured out my life. She took my words and put them in writing. And here they are.

I Am Healing
How do we heal ourselves from being the objects of racism?

I'm telling my story and the process I am going through so you can try it on. I'm doing it now and have been for years.

I'm not through, of course. It's ongoing. But I have figured out how to describe what we are healing from.

The African American Racism System

We all know racism from the White population. All those differences in education and hiring, the percentages in prison, the overall sense of being seen as inferior. As dangerous.

Those stereotypes, however, have been integrated into who we think we are. They have become part of our beliefs about ourselves and behaviors that we have developed into a culture. A system. It has been passed down over generations from slavery, and was added on to in our systemic reactions to the external racism.

I will outline twenty components of the system in Chapter 7, although there are many more.

Section I

Discomfort Being Black

Chapter 1

It's Okay to Heal

Polarization

One way I approached healing was looking at how so many "experts" criticize and blame the opposite side. How this creates polarization. It has caused a world of conflict, of back and forth accusation and criticism, and anger. I was heavily involved in this two-sided look at being Black until I understood that arguing won't change anything.

So I came to understand that I needed to learn how we can talk with each other without taking sides. I am practicing how, and learning more all the time. I'm glad to say that I've gotten pretty good at it.

> *We can talk with each other without taking sides.*

I wasn't always good at it, back when I couldn't see what was going on. Recently I put on a shirt I wore in my old life, and remembered what I was like ten years back. I wanted to gain power by being bigger, stronger, and faster. I thought that the biggest person would have the most power. The most authority. It was an African American norm that I had grown accustom to. But it never felt intuitively right even while I thought I had to go along with it.

I don't do that anymore. I've become my own leader. I practice the opposite of polarization. I've learned how to create an open space, a safe place, where people won't feel judged, where they can just talk. Not surprising, this brings more people to me.

Now I check myself to see how much I'm living in the old self, or how much in the here and now present self. I can get dragged back into the old self when I feel disrespected or think someone might take power over me.

Talking About It

I have a history of inviting friends, students, and clients of all races to ask questions. As I explain what we are going through as human beings, and why we haven't been able to join together to stop racial tension, it helps me understand the disconnect between those of us growing up with the identity of being Black and those who have not lived it. As we understand and heal, I hope the next generation can be relieved of some of the influences.

Self-acceptance

Accepting who I am instead of trying to be someone else is a theme of my healing. Instead of thinking, "Martin Luther King and other leaders did so much," and waiting to step into a role like theirs, I am discovering my own role. I'm not those people. I'm me. Accepting that has freed me to do the

> *Accepting who I am instead of trying to be someone else is a theme of my healing.*

work that is in front of me. Instead of waiting for my moment to come, instead of waiting to be like them, I can continue my journey in my own authenticity.

I'm my own leader

Exposure to several religions helped me get here. I've noticed that when I free myself from dogma I can take in information that helps me understand myself. Who I am, and how I can follow my life as it moves forward. Seeing these religions as potential doorways to spirituality rather than the owners of my spirituality has freed me to find wisdom in the teaching.

Witnessing

When I was growing up I didn't get to see someone who looks like me doing what I wanted to do someday. I thought about the four-minute mile. It was believed that it wasn't possible until someone did it. Then many people did it. When I teach psychology classes to Black future therapists, they see that I did what they want to. They see how I got from where they are to where I am now. This is a fulfilling thought as when early in my career, becoming a therapist and owner of my own practice seemed as impossible as a four-minute mile.

> *When I teach psychology classes to Black future therapists they see how I got from where they are to where I am now.*

It's Okay to Heal

Healing from the massive impact of racism is the

same as breaking the four-minute mile. I did it. I'm doing it. Others can do it. It's okay to heal. It had to start with anger because that was needed for the push forward. Now we can turn to healing.

We are all works in progress, and that's a good thing. It's what makes my life worth living. I get to think about the form I'm making out of this clay.

We React Blindly

White people have been blindly racist, yes. But I had to see how Black people blindly react to situations as if we are helpless. And how this blindness is part of the African American system. Day after day I reflected over my automatic responses when around White people. And I studied the ways that I was changing myself so I could see them for who they are, and react in more rational ways. So I could function out of the system.

When George Floyd was killed by a police officer and Black Lives Matter became a visible movement, I was thrown right into the middle of helping my White friends. Because of my psychology background, along with being Black my whole life, I was able to make sense of it for a lot of people. I got to explain racism in ways I had long understood, but that White people hadn't been interested in. Now they are.

As this event triggered massive understanding of the racism in our country, and in police forces, White friends called me the week after, wanting my input because they didn't understand why Black people needed more than what we had.

They wanted to know how to be a better ally. They didn't feel like they were racists. They knew nothing of covert racism, and the micro-aggressions that are hurtful.

I was glad I had shifted from the angry Black man I was a few years ago so I could talk with them. Back then I would have spoken with resentment. And I wouldn't have been heard. The massive reaction to the police murder of a Black man would have been lost.

Change was going on all around us. The Black Lives Matter movement along with the disruption of the pandemic followed by the economic changes yielded more White people being open to understanding our experience. They are becoming more conscious.

And Black people have an opportunity to relate with White people differently. Giving up the angry Black man mentality offers a chance to understand White naivete, their ignorance, their automatic assumptions learned from the culture. When we live in anger we become unable to use our intuitive abilities, those quiet, sensitive voices that allow us to understand.

> *Giving up the angry Black man mentality offers a chance to understand ignorance and automatic assumptions.*

It's Been Liberating

I looked at my emotional upheaval for what it was, too. Fear of running in my White neighborhood even while feeling accepted by everyone here increased in mid-2020 as the reactivity around me escalated. When I worked out in an open park setting I watched for White people, wondering which side they were on. These fears were stronger after hearing so many conversations about the BLM demonstrations. I became more conscious of them, and then more able to think about what to do.

A Devasting Childhood

I have had the fortune of learning how to heal from a difficult childhood and developing skills that I could then use for healing from racism. Being Black, along with divorcing parents and emotional trauma, I was a devastated child. An angry young Black man.

It started during the divorce when I was around eight. I put on a smiling face, acting like everything was fine while inside it wasn't. I started numbing my emotions, and as years went on I did it more and more. Drugs. Alcohol. Sex. I acted highly extroverted, but really, I was trying to keep everyone at a distance. I was angry all the time. I got in fights just for the sake of expressing it.

> *During the divorce I put on a smiling face, acting like everything was fine and started numbing my emotions.*

Sex as a Drug

When I was young, especially in college, sex was the one way I could feel vulnerable. And it felt good to be the chosen one of the night, it felt empowering and my insecurities would disappear.

But it was momentary. The next day or next week they would come right back. Its real value was only a distraction from what I was feeling.

Being sexually desired is no longer part of my identity. Back then I was going to be the player, the mack, the one sought after. Now my identity is wrapped into other things. My family, being authentic, being real with myself, being able to address what's going on with me. I have a better relationship with myself. When I'm experiencing insecurities in the moment, I'm willing to look at them versus stuffing them down and avoiding them. I no longer need external admiration. I like to be with people who have a particular energy. It's about who a person is which bypasses sexual energy.

I'm committed to my wife in our journey together. That feeds me more than past experiences. Those people weren't liking me, they were embracing the idea of me. The ego image that I put out. And that was the extent of it. Now I have emotional investment.

Cycle Theory

In graduate school studying psychology I started to see what was going on with me. And that there was something I could do about it. I started giving myself time to rest. I didn't go out as much. I developed journaling and meditation. And I stopped criticizing my-

> *Even when I feel like shit I will soon be on the Upside of the Cycle.*

self for dropping into a low place. I knew that I would come back out of it.

I started calling this "Cycle Theory" as a way to see my emotions and behaviors as on a cyclical path. When up and happy, great. And when I drop down into depression or anger, then that's just the way it is. Understanding it as a place on the wave got me to see that even when I feel like shit I remember that I will soon be on the upside of the Cycle. And know that this is just how life is. Everyone Cycles. No one stays on top. And hopefully no one stays on the bottom.

I'm Not Perfect

We can evolve as individuals and as people who no longer respect racism. I don't have the perfect answers as many self-help writers claim to. What I have is the experience of going from a screwed up young person to a husband and father with a good deal of insight. And someone committed to learning year by year. I can't model achieving a perfect life. What I can model is my process of improving myself and improving my life.

> *I went from a screwed up young person to a husband and father with a good deal of insight.*

Chapter 2

The Trauma of Growing up Black

Dr. Joy DeGruy wrote a book called *Post Traumatic Slave Syndrome* (PTSS), which uses the concept of post-traumatic stress disorder, a psychological diagnosis for symptoms of trauma. She is a therapist and college professor who understands how so many of us suffer from what happened to our ancestors. This is known for many after combat, and is now making its way into cultural understanding. DeGruy does a good job showing us why growing up Black causes so many of us to have symptoms of being traumatized.

One of the devastating consequences of being descendants of slaves and living in a racist culture is the difficulty achieving self-esteem. I look at my PTSS as I work on getting out of the box it creates.

Dr. DeGruy wrote:

"Vacant esteem is the state of believing oneself to have no worth, exacerbated by similar pronouncements of inferiority from the personal sphere and larger society. Vacant esteem is the net result of three spheres of influence – society, community, and family. Society influences us through institutions, laws, policies and media. The communities in which we live influence us through establishing norms and encouraging conformity to society at large. Our families encourage us through the ways in which we are raised and groomed to take our place, as our parents see it, in the community and society. When these influences promote a disparaging and limiting identity to which we believe we are confined, vacant esteem can be the result. It is important to note that vacant esteem is a belief about one's worth, not a measure of one's actual worth. Vacant esteem, being a symptom of Post Traumatic Slave Syndrome, is transmitted from generation to generation through the family, community and society."

Here's an example of mine. Psychologist Anne Stirling Hastings (the Anne who assisted with creating this book) contacted me years ago to ask if I would meet with her and a Black man who was writing a book on Black people and therapy. She wanted my input as they worked on putting his book together. They needed therapists to describe their experiences as therapists with Black clients.

I was of course pleased to be involved. And I also I feared being used, actually exploited. I was afraid of being misquoted, of having my words twisted, conveying what I wasn't actually saying. Making me seem extreme. Even vilify me in some way.

I was set up for this by the way Black people are treated by those who don't understand us. And even those who want to. It's also a component of the African American system.

I learned that she was to be trusted but I couldn't start in a place of trust and then stop if warranted. I started from a place of mistrust and then trusted when warranted.

I paid attention to her follow-up questions and the way she respected what I said as true. I am able to reveal anything to her now, knowing it will be respected, although sometimes I have remaining discomfort.

Some therapists might assume that I just have a fear of trusting others. That is unless they are Black and had the same experience with White people. Being told over years that I was exaggerating my experience was traumatizing. For some reason when race is involved people tend to shy away from calling it what it is.

Systemic Racism

Dr. DeGruy said that "African Americans have a unique socialization experience due to centuries of systematic and traumatic programming of inferiority, covering all aspects of being." She says that...."throughout American history....book after book asserted that blacks.... were dirty, lustful, stupid, immoral, and incapable of reasoning."

> *Book after book asserted that blacks.... were dirty, lustful, stupid, immoral, and incapable of reasoning.*

Anne invited me to her house for weekly meditation. One time when I got to the security gate the guard said that he had to call her for a pass as she had forgotten to leave one. When he got her on the phone he then required identification beyond the fact that he had called her on the phone number he had for her. This had not happened to her before. Out of anger she refused. And he refused me entry.

She jumped in her car, drove to the gate and yelled at the guard. She said that he had called her on her phone, and that it makes no sense that he needed further information to prove it was her. She said she was going to report him. He agreed to let me in because, he said, he could see that it was her. This was also not true because he didn't know her personally. He gave in because she was a resident. And because she was White.

I had been ready to leave. I was uncomfortable.

She was able to yell at the guard.

For her, racism was something others experienced. For me it was something I had learned to handle my whole life.

We started talking about systemic racism. She felt outraged over how this is still going on. But this is a whole different thing for me, for someone who has always known it. Now people are awakening to something I tried to make peace with a long time ago. That I am used to.

I've been the one who yelled. But now it's, I just don't want to deal with this today. A numbing feeling took over. I was going there to meditate, not to face being profiled. I just wanted to meditate.

Suppressed Rage
Rage that has built up over the years of my life is harmful. It creates a perpetual cycle, and pushes

me into a victim mentali-
ty. Hypervigilance keeps
me from enjoying life. I

> *I was a victim of
> my own pain.*

am a victim of my own pain. I have to figure out
my physiology each time so I can control it.

Culture Confusion

As I talked with White friends about racism I discovered how some can't understand what Black
people need. I saw that White and Black people
need a bigger picture of how culture has set us
up to think that we are different from each other.

Whites think that having
privilege is just the way
it is. But what has been
missing is understanding

> *Whites think that
> having privilege is
> just the way it is.*

how their ancestors had a struggle too.

Britain sent people over here to get them out of
the country. They struggled to establish a new
country. They created a revolution. The Irish came
here to avoid starvation. They were treated as
inferior. Same with the Italians who arrived in
numbers. And now as Mexicans and Central and
South Americans are immigrating and seeking
asylum, some are adapting and changing their
identity from outsiders to part of the culture.

When I think back on how each nationality had
to struggle to integrate by becoming White, I see
parallels with how slave offspring are pushed to
do this. Pushed to let go of our culture of struggle and resilience.

American Privilege

My wife came from Russia at age eighteen with

nothing, worked two jobs, put herself through college and sent money home. It helps me acknowledge my own privilege from being raised in this country even with my own burdens. I'm an American. I didn't have to immigrate. I can appreciate many people with a higher level of privilege than I have. Seeing the other side helps my healing process.

Peace Begins With Me

I can create a different scene. But I had to get out of my victim mentality. Based on movies and TV and the culture, if you

> *I'm finding it difficult to put this information out there to be read.*

weren't an athlete or a rapper you were going to be a gang banger. A drug dealer. It's portrayed in so many ways. Or I could be in the military. That's acceptable.

I was told by a high school friend that I couldn't be prom king because I was Black. He wasn't being mean. He thought it was true. So I became prom king. I just wanted to prove people wrong. I spent so much of my life trying to prove people wrong. The underdog mindset gave me purpose when I had doubt in myself.

The momentum of anger carried me for a long time but then I didn't know how to be. I stopped being the underdog, but I still didn't know how to be the thriver, the achiever. I didn't know because I had always been that person who was, "Fuck you, I'm going to prove you wrong." I didn't know how to make the switch from trying to run the race after everybody else, to just staying in my own lane.

I wanted to fight. I would go out looking for fights because I didn't know what else to do. I needed to express it somehow, to get it out of me.

> *I would go out looking for fights because I needed to express anger.*

I was lucky to be an athlete from a small town. I didn't want to go to college in a city, as I knew I would get in more trouble there. San Luis Obispo was more like home. I wouldn't have been able to stay out of trouble in a city. I still did get in trouble, but nowhere near as much as I could have.

I'm a lot calmer now, but most young men don't have a scholarship like I did. They don't have a trajectory. My parents pushed me about college, they were really on it. I do see how lucky I was because it gave me time. I could move to a city after years in San Luis Obispo. I learned how to stop making stupid decisions. I was getting better at being productive in my own life rather than having it dictated for me.

Ever-Present Anger

This is the title of a section in the book *Post Traumatic Slave Disorder* by Joy DeGruy. While I thought I was enraged all the time because my life was influenced by racism and by my particular childhood, DeGruy paints the picture of how the life styles in slavery also created it.

She says, "…there is a wellspring of anger that lies below the surface of many African Americans and it doesn't take much for it to emerge and be expressed." She stated my exact experience. She

> *A wellspring of anger doesn't take much to emerge.*

goes on to say, "The ever-present anger is one of the most pronounced behavior patterns associated with the Post Traumatic Slave Syndrome."

DeGruy explains how anger is the *normal* response to a blocked goal. The healthy use of anger can unblock goals, or shift to a new direction. However Blacks have been blocked for centuries. She also explains how White people modeled anger and violence toward slaves, and they picked this up.

"Even when we're feeling good an ever-present anger resides just below the surface: anger at the violence, degradation, and humiliation visited upon us, our ancestors, and our children; anger at being relegated to the margins of the society in which we live; and at the misrepresentation and trivialization of our history and culture; and finally, anger at living in the wealthiest nation in the world and not having equal opportunity to its riches."

She ends by saying that understanding this anger can lead to exploration of how to transform it into something useful and productive.

This is my focus, of course. I have been lucky enough to have parents and a life in which I am able to heal my PTSS.

What to do With Anger

I'm discovering what to do with the anger we all have. First I learned how to not cause myself problems. I can calm myself. But we need to be able to do more. We need a way to join with each other and shed it out of us.

> *I can calm myself.*

First we have to remove the shame embedded in our souls so we don't see ourselves the way they do. If I am denied entrance to a gated community I can just notice that this person is profiling. I no longer feel shame and anger over it. I do not internalize their negative beliefs. I am in a mindset that I have done nothing wrong.

Our Music Empowers Us

Listening to Kendrick Lamar's song, DNA, is like hearing my heart talk. Hearing my heart literally speak. It's a battle cry. An acknowledgement of what's real. I've been told all these negative things about myself, about my DNA and my skin. And then I hear of the accomplishments of people who have my skin tone, how they rise above. I feel invincible when I hear that song.

Hearing someone from my generation talk about my experience that I can't articulate lets me feel that I am not alone. And that I have more power than I give myself credit for. And I need to use it.

One of Lamar's songs says that Black men get quiet by age thirty. No longer putting out their opinion, not being hot blooded, hot tempered, saying that something is wrong.

By the age of thirty I was married with two children, and I didn't want anything bad to happen to my family. I didn't want to deal with the bullshit any more. I didn't want to represent something that causes threat. I just wanted to live my fucking life.

I don't have to dissect the lyrics, I just feel them. Even though you and I may be from different walks of life we experience the same thing. It's in our race and our bloodlines. The lyrics come from traumatic experience which now has to be healed.

It's history of what's happening.

The rawness in music is what has motivated me. I still go back to 2Pac. "Keep Your Head Up" is one of my favorite songs and my anthem for surviving my first years of college. It's talking about how keeping your head up gets you through to a brighter day. He was only twenty-six when he died

> *Music is their playbooks for how to get through life.*

yet his impact has been global. What would have happened if he was still alive? His music and political discourse is still relevant today. This music gave me a different way to navigate. It's their playbooks for how they were getting through life. They have been powerfully helpful.

Mainstream has promoted toxic material and tried to label it hip-hop. Some artists have lost touch with the lineage they come from and cannot compare to the oldest G's in hip-hop. The traditional forms of storytelling are education for Black people. It's verbal communication.

You don't just hear the information. You feel the information.

> *You feel the information*

I feel comfortable in this culture when I don't feel comfortable most of the time. I listen to 2Pac, Nas, and KRS-1 when pursuing knowledge of self and environment. Ice Cube, Common, and Wu-Tang Clan taught me how to *"Diversify my [your] Bonds"* when it comes to my talents, finances, and community. Snoop-Dogg, E-40, and 50 Cent all taught me to have confidences in my swagger and to not be deterred.

Kendrick Lamar and J-Cole help me walk to the beat of my own drum. As I hear two brothers from my generation continuing to express their art form while they take their own steps to evolve is uplifting. They give me the motivation to continue to live life my way.

Losing DMX this year was difficult as his albums were the background music to most of my teenage years. His own struggle with mental health help me normalize my own. His song "Slippin" pulled me out of depressive states. To quote Lupe Fiasco "Hip Hop Save my life."

Bob Marley is a Saint

Our Rhythm is not one dimensional. It can be felt across the seas. Bob Marley's language is love. Good vibrations. He was awake to what was going on with Malcom X, Martin Luther King, and more. He was a rebel. The art form of reggae is powerful when you can hear the mix of soul R&B with the island feel. Bob Marley was able to take the rage of our ancestors and distill it into a language of love that can be heard and felt.

Chapter 3

My History of Racism

I went to a private high school on the other side of town, a more affluent side, and there were times I got stopped at six in the morning on the way to weight lifting. They asked, "what are you doing on this side of town?"

There it was, a Wednesday morning. I had the name of the school in huge letters on the front of my shirt. I told them where I was going, that it's right down the street. I had to be calm even in my outrage. I've had to subdue my outrage for so long that sometimes it's aggravating to see that other people get to have it.

Other people get to have outrage.

When I was in high school the cops talked respectfully most of the time because I had learned from my police officer father to talk to them that way. I knew how to calm them down. But why was it my job to calm them down? To make them feel okay so they reduced their profiling of me?

In a bar in San Luis Obispo another guy and I got mouthy, and he said, "see you outside." We got in a fight, and two other guys jumped in. We were rolling around on the ground in a very public area when the bars were closing down.

When the cops showed up I immediately raised my hands in the air. I started yelling, "I am not resisting. I am not resisting." I sat down on the curb with my hands still up, continuing to yell, "I am not resisting."

The two guys that had joined in ran off, but the guy I was fighting was on the ground. He swung at the officer. They could see how drunk he was. As they took him to the side, I said again that I wasn't resisting. I slowed myself down. I've learned that if I can speak about it they will be more willing to listen. I often think about what would have happened if I had swung at the officers. Would I have become another statistic?

I could calm myself because of what I learned from being a track athlete. Breathing is an integral part of it. I had to learn to see what is going on right now inside of me to do my best.

I paid attention to every inhale and exhale. I knew how to focus on my body when preparing myself for an athletic scholarship at a Div 1 college. Now I could use that skill for a different situation.

I discovered that when I don't focus on breathing, I start reacting. I clench up. My hands tighten into fists and I get angry. Focusing on breathing may seem counterintuitive as it is common to clench the body in times of stress.

> *When I don't focus on breathing, I clench up. My hands tighten into fists. Breathing may seem counterintuitive.*

When Usain Bolt is setting world records in the 100m Dash his hands and body are lose, he is breathing, and he seems relaxed going across the finish line. This body awareness and visualizations were steps in building my mindfulness practice.

My dad, a deputy chief police officer, taught me that you will always encounter assholes in your life. He said to talk to them with some sense of respect, actually talk to every person with a sense of respect even if you don't respect how they go about their lives. When having some sense of another human being, talking with them can calm them. For him that came from having to talk people down from doing violent aggressive things.

I came from a diverse family so I got to see a lot of variety. Some were in law enforcement, some were affluent. Some in gangs, others were first responders. Multiple veterans of Vietnam and Iraq. By having a diverse family I was able to see how different people lived their lives. I could get advice and feedback from many walks of life rather than thinking life had to be one way. This gave me an edge in being able to learn from other's mistakes. I was able to learn and apply their experience to my own struggles.

I Struggle

After one of Anne's and my meetings I wasn't able to separate my raw emotions from my acceptable ones. I had poured out my feelings along with the facts of my whole life. I had to see what my life was like. And what it is like.

I have an emotional screen up most of the time and when it drops I feel the pain that it holds

> *When my emotional screen drops I feel the pain that it holds off.*

off. The screen is valuable a lot of the time, like when I use it to push away anger that isn't appropriate. But it also shows up to protect me from feelings that are better let out.

One form of the screen is overthinking before deciding what to say to people. And that layer isn't just mine. Barak Obama and Michael Jordan talk about having to be the ideal Black person. Or the Black person safe to talk to.

People see me as a safe Black person so they are willing to ask questions. I do it so that a White person may feel less racist. But I wish for the relief of letting it out, of being loud. There aren't a lot of people I feel safe having my feelings in front of.

When I went across town to a school with wealthier White people I got to know them as human beings. I got to know the privilege they had, and also the struggle they had with that privilege.

Yet even recently when I was profiled at a security gate, Anne saw that I flattened my energy. I just said that I'm used to it. I used long practiced methods of sidestepping when I had been profiled once again.

I saw how I do that, thinking it feels better than being angry one more time. Just wanting to have a nice meditation at Anne's house. But I want people to be able to know about it because that's what's helped me.

I've yelled, kicked things, screamed, and called people racist. I've done it to people's faces. At this

> *I've yelled, kicked things, and called people racist.*

point I see that it isn't productive because the message gets lost in anger.

When I was younger I was all about Malcom X when he was in his mindset of anger. You're going to feel my rage if you bring that hostility or violence toward me. I didn't understand how Martin Luther King stayed in a love mentality. It seemed so weak. Now I see how much strength is in it.

It's not generally known that late in his life Malcom X refined his original message. He still believed in black power, but his focus was brotherhood. He believed that White people could be allies. This was after he had made his pilgrimage to Mecca and saw men of all races and ethnicities worshiping and communing together. Black people would need to own who we really are rather than believing the story we have been told of who we are .

I think that's where I'm at. Not pressed down so much. I'm working on understanding and using the MLK mentality. But I had to stop squashing anger, and I had to stop replacing it with denial and apathy.

I had feelings that weren't seen and I thought about a lot. I felt crazy when things were going through my mind that others didn't see. If I were to say it out loud I would feel crazy. But when I read about those who did stand up and took the brunt of the civil rights movements, I gain strength.

There has been progress. Now it is time for healing. We can heal our-

> *Now it is time for healing.*

selves. We can stop living in survival, pushing feelings down until we have another explosion.

Fear

I use to carry a knife because I was afraid of losing my body. I finally gave up my fear of death by seeing my body as a vessel for my mind. When I freed myself I know that no one can take control of my mind. I no longer carry a knife.

Rubin Hurricane Carter was a heavy weight champion falsely convicted of murder and imprisoned for many years until finally proven innocent. He said that no one could imprison his mind. He wrote a book about it, and a young man who read it took on proving him innocent. A movie was made of his life played by Denzel Washington. A quote from when he was in solitary confinement still rings in my head. "You can't break me, because you didn't make me."

I learned about him when I was twelve. I knew I had to take on his approach. It was profound to see his strength and it helped me develop much of my mindset.

Anxiety and Panic Attacks

I had anxiety my whole life but I didn't know what it was. I was just

I didn't know how to describe anxiety.

told to quit crying. Hunker down. I didn't know how to describe the sensation.

Early in my learning about it I went to an outdoor public gym in red shorts and no shirt and several Hispanic men set out to intimidate me. I was doing pushups, and my tattoos showed that

I was from the North. They talked among themselves in a way to threaten me. Part of me started reacting in the old ways. I knew what was going to happen next. I would fight. I could feel the tension in my neck, the clenched breath as that familiar feeling of danger, started to play out in my mind.

Then I had a moment of clarity. I thought about what I had done to succeed. I was in graduate school. I asked myself, was it worth it to jeopardize that in this moment? Because it would have been a fight. They started to move around so that I couldn't see all of them. The memories of being jumped earlier in my life surged into my consciousness.

So I finished what I was doing, put my head phones in, and took off. Having been a track athlete I knew I could outrun them. When I got to my apartment I broke down. My whole body shook. Adrenalin seeped out of me. I had to take a cold shower to catch my breath.

It wasn't my first panic attack, but it was the first time I realized that it was a panic attack. It was an all-consuming sensation throughout my body. I had them when I got in fist fights, but back then I could drink. I could smoke something. But I didn't have anything in my apartment, and I had no money.

So I had to write about it. I had to get all the shame pieces out. Self-judgment ran through my mind, like, "You were a bitch, you didn't fight them, you didn't take them on." And I had to admit how often I had to be the tough guy. I had to prove that I was "Black enough." That I wouldn't be messed with.

The panic showed what was constantly going on in my mind and body. I was vigilant, always expecting to be jumped, always ready to fight and win.

Stopped by Police

Shortly after that I got stopped by the police when walking to grad school. They were looking for a suspect that matched my description even though I had my backpack on. A cop pulls up, jumps out with his gun drawn, and asked my name.

I held on as my heart was jumping out of my chest. I wanted to reach for my wallet, I wanted to do so many things. I just held on. I said, "My name is L.J." He asked me if my name was the name of the suspect, and I said, "No, my name's L.J." He put his gun down, but he asked me where I was going. I said "Grad school, do you want to see my fucking books? Do you need to see my ID? What the fuck do you want from me?"

People had gathered around, so I had witnesses to feel safe talking to him like that.

He's like, sorry about that, wrong person. His partner learned that they found the actual suspect.

I was on my way to a class where we were studying multicultural psychology. We were talking about color blindness and how it causes harm. One woman believed that it was a good thing in that it meant she wasn't racist. She saw people for who they are, not their color.

I opened my mouth to explain how that dismisses my whole experience. "If I were your client I would never come back because saying you are color blind dismisses my existence. And it's not your fault because it's what you were taught. It blocks out what I went through just twenty minutes ago."

I really had to talk about it. And I did. With adrenalin still pumping, I described what had just happened. I am grateful to the professor who encouraged me to talk rather than hold it back from fear of creating a divide or overwhelming my class mates.

Racism is Traumatizing

It was an interesting year in grad school because I was learning what goes on in my body. I learned to understand trauma, especially how racism is trauma.

The overt forms such as name calling and putting us down as inferior are becoming visible in our culture. The covert kinds are less so. The suspicion in stores, the profiling that people don't realize they are doing. And a long list of beliefs about us that people think are true. I don't eat watermelon and fried chicken around others to avoid fitting a stereotype. My friend had said I was not eligible to be homecoming king because of my color. This is all traumatizing. Even the positive ones. How often are we provoked into acting a specific way to prove our blackness or to dismantle a stereotype?

I would like White people to think about how to approach someone with the desire to not traumatize them. It's about something they can do,

> *Can White people approach us with the desire to not traumatize?*

or not do. I've talked with White friends and saw how useful it is for them to think about it like this.

I explained it in class so the woman who said she was color blind could understand. Covert racism traumatizes the recipient. I included that those who have been taught color blindness were trying to deal with racism, not understanding that their desire to not be racist was not helping.

Educating White People

After the murder of George Floyd when I began talking with White friends, I explained that it wasn't just Black or White. There was police brutality, and media coverage, and the pandemic and economic issues. I could explain that this was a systemic problem that never gets fully addressed because we (humans) are so quick to put everyone in a box.

I got to hear what other people are thinking, and I got to say what I had seen for so many years. The idea that I have to be better to be perceived as equal, that I have to work to be seen as non-threatening. This runs through all of our veins, and brings frustration and anger.

I wonder how much should I say, and how do I say it in a way that doesn't scare people off.

> *There are truths hidden in American history.*

When I describe truths that have been hidden in American history I might get negative reactions.

We aren't taught this in school. We White wash history. We say we're in America where bad things don't happen. I'm afraid I'll sound like a conspiracy theorist. Or seen as just bad mouthing the country. This is so not true.

I want to be able to celebrate our traditions because there are reasons why we have them. But we have to know the whole truth and become comfortable with it.

I was asked about the protest and violence. They wanted to know who was going to stand up and be the leader. This was even after Colin Kaepernick took a knee during the national anthem, which claims we are all free, to draw awareness to police brutality. He was not the only athlete who did this. He was vilified as unpatriotic and against our troops. Before him Tommie Smith and John Carlos had their gold and silver medals taken away for raising their fists during the medal ceremony for the 1968 Olympics, even though they had earned the right to speak for their community.

I got to say how our leaders who were killed may have only a paragraph in history books. Their killing was a message to anyone who wanted to confront racism. Like the one slave who stepped out was killed to as an example to everyone one else to not stand out.

We are not taught about these moments in history because they create a dissonance between what we believe the country stands for and what we are practicing. This is why these conversations are needed to move society forward.

Trauma
A friend in college told me that I had experienced a lot of trauma, and that being Black added so

much more. So I started looking at the physiology of it, and what it had done to me.

It helped to understand how so much is harmful, not normal as I had made it out to be. She pointed out that being always tense and alert is hyper-vigilance, that these are trauma responses. I started to work on myself. I started the healing process. I started letting go of ego-driven hardness and started to heal my body.

Yoga was an early tool to help me start. It was cheap, and I could do it anywhere. I learned to let go of body tension. My mood elevated from being in less physical pain.

> *Yoga was cheap, and I could do it anywhere.*

Chapter 4

A Black Man in Prison

As is well known, the percentage of Black people in prison is much higher than White people. I was lucky enough to avoid being prosecuted for law breaking so I didn't go to prison. However, my friend, Donovan Wedington, did. He has written a book of his experiences as an addict who went to prison at age twenty. It's about how therapy helped him, and explained how this could be more integrated into Black culture. He gave me permission to put his prison experience here.

Prison Dungeon

The culture shock of prison is staggering. You're in a world you know nothing about. You have nothing in common, you have no friends, no backup, no family. The level of shame that comes from being on a prison bus shackled like a slave to the next man, is palatable. The prison guards and police officers don't even see you as human. It's as if you're a dog, and not a good dog either. You're an old broken down mutt that just keeps shitting on the lawn, digging holes, and knocking trash cans over. And every time you try to feed it, it bites.

You have this knowing that if you get out of line the beating could be bad. These guys are begging you to make a move. My awareness is hyper intense. My freeze response is fired and in full effect. There's no fighting and there's no fleeing.

Needless to say the bus ride was extremely quiet. Just a few guys spoke, more than likely ones who had been there before.

I could hear my heartbeat In my head. First you see the gate with that sharp barbwire, that 20 foot high gate. And then you see the stone walls. It looks like an old Scottish castle dungeon.

As you exit the bus you hear the unforgettable prison echo, the sound of a thousand angry men, that clang of iron bars mixed with the grunts of mass weights being lifted. Each man working to maintain the illusion of physical supremacy.

San Quentin is California State's Receiving and Distribution Prison. Every level criminal are all mixed together for the first 3 to 5 months before being processed and shipped out to their appropriate level detention center. At the receiving block where you're assigned your prison number you are stripped naked and powdered down, as another man makes you spread of your butt in front of a hundred others.

Entering San Quentin is cut into my memory. The site of the orange jumpsuits, plain white socks with tan slippers. The smell of tops-rolled cigarettes and toilet paper incense, the talking of a thousand men echoes off the seven-story stonewalls. I can still feel the cold concrete and the coarse hard cotton socks from the laundry.

To this day I've never seen more blacks in one area in my entire life. It was a sea of African Americans for hundreds of yards.

From corner to corner were black man. Young, old and everything in between. I asked this kid who looked extremely young how old he was. He said 16....

What, I shouted. How is that even possible?

He explained the how and why of it but I can't recall the details. I do however remember the age. Sixteen! How did he end in up in here........Why are so many of us here....these questions ran through my mind. It wasn't answered for a long time.

From *Why Don't African Americans go to Therapy and Why I did.* Unpublished manuscript.

As a therapist I have worked with Black men who have been traumatized by the prison system and expected to function "normally" once they get out. Coming out can be just as traumatizing, and then you are expected to not talk about or process the atrocities seen.

> *Black men traumatized by the prison system are expected to function "normally."*

To have no control over your life and wellbeing, and then have a permanent mark on you even after the time served, is not rehabilitating. It's another form of slavery.

Chapter 5

Shame

What is Shame?

When I was immersed in healing, Anne asked me to read two of her books when still in the manuscript stage. Both were on shame. *Shedding Shame and Claiming Freedom: How to Eradicate Our Most Painful Emotion* describes the feeling itself, where it comes from, and how we manage it. It makes sense of so many of our emotions and behaviors.

Next came *Shedding Shame Workbook: Release the Cause of Depression, Anxiety and Lack of Self-Care.* These books helped me see some of the underpinning of the harm trauma causes. I got to read them when they were in manuscript form and use the vital information in them. She put a quote of mine on the back of each!

Here is some of what Anne wrote about shame and the ways that we try to not feel it:

> You know what shame feels like, that hot face, skin crawling sensation that makes you want to be anywhere else. The intense wanting to make the other person wrong, to affirm that they are wrong about you. And those bad feelings you have about yourself, that you don't deserve self-care, perhaps even being alive. The embarrass-

ment when you make a mistake, when you did something you feel is wrong. Those secrets that you don't want anyone to know about you. The sick, shaky feeling of being found out. Losing when compared with others regarding money, work, education, and looks. The desire to be seen as a good person even though feeling like you don't deserve self-esteem.

Humanness brings with it the right to belong in a community and develop ourselves to the fullest. No one is on the outside. Shame can interfere with knowing this. The person who feels unworthy will feel as if they are not entitled to belong.

Then there are the many ways you avoid feeling it. Drinking, working too much, being busy, talking on and on, achieving in order to prove yourself, addictions, and the big one – shaming others. Criticizing others, gossiping, looking down on. People who buy what they can't afford, or gamble compulsively, or shop addictively, or focus on wanting what they can't have are suffering from shame that prevents understanding that we all deserve true belonging.

This emotion distorts us so much that it brings about a long list of personal and social distortions. Hatred, revenge, racism, sexism, addictions, rape, child molestation, child abuse, cruelty, economic recessions, parenting difficulties, lying, employment conflicts, marital problems, most mental illness, and absurd reasoning by banks and stock purchasers based on greed, are caused by shame. *They are all caused by our loving humanness interrupted by shame followed by countless methods of avoiding shame, resulting in the blind harming of every one of us.* Shame is the underlying culprit that has to be healed in order for everything else to work well. World peace cannot be obtained by political changes. It will only come when each one of us takes on the task of finding our integrity, and the painful healing of shame to obtain it.

From *Shedding Shame Workbook: Release the Cause of Depression, Anxiety and Lack of Self-Care.*

It helped to understand the difference between the feeling of shame, and the ways that I sought to stop the feeling of it. I did this with anger at anyone

> *When I got someone to feel inferior I could temporarily stop feeling inferior.*

who wanted to treat me badly, even fighting to show that I was better. I was trying to stop feeling shame for being Black. When I got someone to feel inferior I could temporarily stop feeling inferior.

Shame for Being Black Brings on Shaming

Black people are shame loaded, and it gets others to shame us. It becomes our identity. When we walk towards a White person believing they are judging us, and we feel shame for that, we exude shame. And they perceive it without understanding why they feel the way they do.

Anne told me about a woman at her dog park who lost her arm from the elbow down, yet doesn't cover it up. She is so absent of shame that Anne had no reaction to seeing a stump on the woman's arm. She compared that to how we usually feel when seeing that. We don't want to look. We see the person as defective in some way. Instead Anne watched how she managed her two dogs with one hand and a bracelet on the shortened arm. Because the woman had no shame no one there was triggered into our usual reactions around those who feel shame about themselves.

When Black people feel no shame or fear when around White people the same is true. They are less likely to be triggered into seeing us as different. As belonging in a different category of humanity. My White friends have told me of their other Black friends and how they react to them differently because of this.

From a Black Community to a White One

My college, Cal Poly (California Polytechnic State University) is a predominantly White school in a White town on the coast of California. I chose it from among the scholarships I was offered because it was one of the top state schools in California, and it was in nature.

When talking with a girl at the first party I went to, she said, "What sport do you play?" I didn't look different from other students other than I was Black. I wasn't showing my muscles or anything. In one way it was a compliment because I got here on my athletic abilities. But I also had high grades. I was smart too. The hard part was automatically being seen as an athlete. I took this to mean that its's all we Black students are capable of. It's in the African American system definition of us. Why wasn't I proud of my ability to complete the grueling process of developing my athletic talent in order to compete at the college level?

If I'm perceived as a shame-worthy person, as lesser-than, then I will likely do something to defend against that shame. Shedding critical beliefs about ourselves that prevent getting to our vulnerable feelings can allow change. I have been able to go to therapy, talk it through, and see that that seed has been there for a long time. It wasn't until I graduated with my Master's degree that I started to actually believe I was smart.

Slave Downloading of Shame

We have had our DNA programmed for us to act and feel certain ways.   Mental health discovered this when Holocaust survivors' children went to therapy with symptoms of being survivors. Dr. Bruce Lypton is a molecular biologist who wrote *The Wisdom of Cells*,

> The Wisdom of Cells, *and* The Biology of Belief *show how our DNA can be programed.*

and *The Biology of Belief*. He gives a clear understanding of how our DNA can be programed.

Can you imagine what it was like for kids to grow up in a relatively normal family here in the US and then find themselves throwing up when reading about the killing of a helpless adult? Or when working all day physically exerting and when getting home, fighting off sobs? Or waking up in the morning feeling as if you have no life and might as well die?

This is common for people whose parents lived through the reality. Even though it makes no sense now.

Then the third generation survivors carry trauma that hasn't been released by the two generations above them. A client of Anne's had panic attacks when driving by LAX (Los Angeles International Airport.) He was afraid that cop cars would flood onto the freeway, forcing cars to the tarmac and the people onto planes. This is clearly an irrational fear. He and Anne were able to make sense of it when he talked about how two of his grandparents were shuttled from a work camp onto a train headed for a death camp. They knew they were on their way to being killed. The war ended before the train reached its goal.

The level of trauma his grandparents felt was too great for them to resolve so it was passed onto their children. Those children were also unable to resolve it so they passed it on to the grandson.

Apparently it is easier for those who downloaded it to release it as after talking about it three times he can drive right past LAX with no fear.

Releasing Ancestors' Trauma

I breathed a sigh of relief when learning that some of what we do is because our slave ancestors had done it or felt it. Now I have a way to look at my actions through that lens. When I think about dangers I am in I can check back to my slave history.

> *Some of what we do is because of our slave ancestors*

And of course separate out real dangers because of being Black in a racist culture, versus parts of the inherited trauma that continues to keep me in survival mindset.

I'm not saying this has been easy. I see it as an ongoing practice, as questions to ask myself so that I don't think there's something wrong with me when I don't want to do something good for myself. There's nothing wrong with me, instead I'm acting like a slave ancestor who had good reason to feel the way I do now.

I watched a talk about how Black women tend to downplay their children's abilities. They showed a White woman telling a Black mother how good her son was in school, and his special gifts. The mother shrugged it off, dismissing it.

In our culture the general idea is that being best is a good thing. You win. So why would a mother dismiss her child like that? We could examine the psychological reasons from her childhood, or how she splits her children into those deserving compliments from those who deserve being put down.

But if we take that approach then we can never look at the DNA downloading this mother may have had. It makes no sense now, but back when the outstanding child was sold, the mother would have tried to downplay his talents. Make him out to be ordinary and not worth buying.

I shook my head as I pondered which of if my stressful emotions weren't from this life at all. And those who say they're from a past life are probably wrong too. A likely source of fear and trauma reactions and ways of handling them are from the hideousness of slavery.

Where Our Trauma Emotions Come From

When I was a teen I read about slave experiences all the time. It was all I would read. So I have a good knowledge of what the people went through. And now I understand some of what I downloaded.

Then I learned to meditate. It changes our brain waves and allows information to appear along with internal awareness.

So when I want to understand an emotion that doesn't seem to make sense, I close my eyes and just pay attention. Sometimes all that happens is that I become peaceful. But other times I see movies. It may have happened to my ancestors, but even if it didn't, it lets me see what might have happened that now makes me feel like this. Even if the movie isn't entirely right it doesn't matter. I have a sense of it based on an understanding of slave life. And it frees me to think that I don't have to do it anymore.

Now that sounds easy, but it isn't an intellectual process. I had to feel, and then connect that with what may have actually happened, and then see if I *feel* a connection.

Downloaded Shame

We are shame loaded, aren't we? The objects of racism. That horrible feeling of being somehow defective, even thinking we belong to a

> *We are shame-loaded objects of racism.*

defective race, and then being mad about it. As I challenged that belief I looked at what had been set up more than four hundred years ago.

One example is my feelings about being educated and in a profession which few Black people are. While it makes sense that I might feel some guilt for doing better than others, my feelings are a lot more than that.

Going to college on an athletic scholarship is acceptable because we are allowed to be strong and athletic as slaves were valued for being strong. We were more useful. So the culture lets us be successful that way. We let ourselves be successful that way.

But after completing my education I became a professional, then an academic.

I thought about what it was like for slaves who stood out. The house slaves that cooked and took care of the children ate better. And dressed better. The smart ones were taught how do tasks beyond working in the fields. They wouldn't have belonged. They couldn't fit in. And now I look like I'm living a White life, married to a White woman with White-looking kids. I fit in with my family, but the shame of being different lives in me.

When meditating I "saw" my ancestor working around the plantation mansion, and eventually sitting at a desk in an outbuilding working on business finances. His intelligence had been observed, and the staff used him for repetitive tasks. He stood out from the other slaves, and was shamed by them for it. And now I feel shamed for having advanced education and a well-paying profession.

Most downloaded experience is of physical harm and family separation. Beatings. Required level of work. Children sold. Couples separated. Women used for breeding.

I was angered in college classes when told that many slaves weren't treated badly. They were well-fed livestock. I know

> *We were told that many slaves weren't treated badly.*

that the very existence of being owned and seen as livestock is so damaging that even if some slave owners were good to them, I will not minimize the overall horror of a human being owned by another human.

What do we do now?
We learn about slave owning. We think about what kind of treatment our ancestors might have had. And we think about how they felt. How much shame. Fear. Loss of loved ones.

And we compare our own experience of life.

Or start the other way around. Think about your present experience of life. Do you feel loss and shame and fear that makes no sense? Take that back to how you think slaves may have felt that way, and why. Think about how they were stuck with those emotions – and how you aren't.

When I feel threatened, most of the time I stop and reflect. Sometimes I can't if the feelings are so strong that I think they must be about me,. As I imagine an ancestor, I breathe. I move slowly. I use the exercises I have discovered are useful when distressed. Fighting makes no sense. Running doesn't either. And freezing is pretty useless. But now I can pull myself into the present. I have tools.

The best part is that I know I am cleaning out that downloaded history – all those feelings that aren't created in the present.

Some of My Shame

When I traced it back in time I remembered when my parents were divorcing, and my idea of family changed. There was a lot of back and forth when I was the messenger. That was the first time I didn't feel strong enough to put things together. I lived in the feeling of shame. My reality was breaking. It haunted me even though I put on a good soldier face. Once I was in grad school studying psychology, I started noticing this thing that I do every year, the excessive numbing every November. Excessive drinking and smoking, and extroversion, even though I was trying to keep everyone away from me.

I started to shed that reaction. I gave myself space to rest more, to take care of myself. I used my tools of journaling and meditation. When I'm on that lower side I became able to accept feeling depleted. The Down Cycle. I'm no longer afraid that it won't go back up.

Questioning Religion

Children are taught the religion their family follows, and they soak it up. As children, we are trying to understand the world we have just come into.

> *Children soak up the religion their family follows, but might become stuck in it.*

But we might become stuck in that definition of ourselves instead of being open to new information.

Christianity was instilled in me at an early age when my parents were divorcing. Everything was chaotic, and so most of the time I was at church. Even with this exposure somehow I wasn't prevented from allowing new information in.

I felt the need to question my teachers. Not thinking they were wrong, just to question. I can't go along with anything unquestioned. It's allowed me to think well in unusual situations.

From studying and practicing several religions I found that all of them have harmful elements,

> *All religions have harmful elements, and all have value.*

and all of them have value. So I didn't just accept that what my parents said was right. Or what pastors said.

The pastor of one church told us that George Bush was ordained by God to be in the place he was after 911. They quoted the Book of Revelations where it says towers will fall as the beginning of the apocalypse. Hearing this at age twelve changed my perspective of Christianity. These ideas did not make sense to me even at that age. I started to understand the power of fear-mongering.

And there was corruption in the church. A pastor bought a plane with a building fund to commute to the new church being built. We were told that God wanted this purchase to happen. This did not make sense to me either.

One time when we were praying I found myself envisioning a Muslim teenager about my age In Iraq. I "saw" him going through his prayer rituals like I was. I was stunned at the pride and peaceful nature of his practice. I could see the beauty of his culture.

In that moment a thought came to me. If my God is all powerful and all knowing, why would he condemn this faithful Muslim teen? He is probably more committed to his practices than I am to mine. Why would he be punished for being a good human? A good neighbor.

I realized that my spiritual beliefs did not fit with religion. I realized religions could be powerful tools to awaken spirituality, but no one has control over my spirit. I had to abandon dogma and instead discover what was right for me.

Don't Blame White People

There aren't many truly racist people now except for those who identify as White supremacists. Most racism is coming from fear or ignorance.

Blaming someone who's ignorant is a waste of energy. I want to know, instead, if I can be open enough to understand where they are coming from. Can I hear them?

I want to help people feel safe enough to talk about their beliefs. And then sit

> *Don't Blame White People*

with discomfort as I explain what I, as a Black man, have gone through. Where I can say, "When you say that, this is what comes up for me." And then talk about my experience. When I bring myself into it without blaming, without shaming, just saying "this is my experience," the listener might take it in.

We can contradict some of the assumptions about all Black people. If you're not able to talk about it then they miss out. This curiosity around racist stuff is too valuable for us to ignore.

If we come at them with anger then they become defensive and miss the message. So I'm precise in how I do this. I channel the energy and presence of James Baldwin and Fredrick Douglass, master orators and debaters who could deliver their truth about racism while still keeping their White audiences empathetically engaged.

I had to get through my anger first, though. As I grew up I found out about racism, and learned how to manage it. In my twenties my rage came out because I was exhausted from having to be a certain way. And felt shame if I weren't. I had to be courteous, I had to be kind. I had to change the bass in my voice so people felt comfortable around me. I did "code switching" where I change my language to fit the work environment, or talking with colleagues, or with Black friends.

When employed I couldn't call out the microaggressions and negative assumptions. I had to smile and nod. Those who know me personally know I can be loud and my laughter heard, but it took time to be comfortable being myself at work. I don't change myself much anymore. I had to be able to, though. I empathize for those who are still in situations that keep them locked in this cycle of non-acceptance of self.

When I had my hair in corn rows I would eventually shave them off. I was programmed to not accept my own look, and so much of myself. That inhibited the use of my intuitive ability to connect for a long time.

There was a time when I couldn't go out without smoking weed. Not every day, but when going to a party, and with a few drinks. I faced this unhealthy use back then, and even now need to look at my relationship with substances. I have to examine, alright, am I having a little too much wine this month? Am I starting to use it as a go-to rather than using better self-care mechanisms? This is not to vilify cannabis, it's to point out that anything used in excess can become toxic even if its original purpose was to help in some way.

I am grateful I had this to cope, and I realize as I grew, my tools for selfcare grew as well. Instead of looking at teens as addicts, let's see how it's a copying strategy or self-medication for emotional pain.

When camping with my wife and kids I had a panic attack when seeing a Confederate flag. I went

> *I panicked when seeing a Confederate flag.*

straight to my old self, searching for the knife I no longer carry. Thoughts ran through my head in lightning speed. "I need to stay awake, where are my kids? What do I need to do, who the fuck has that flag?" My heart started to seize up as I became ready to fight. I felt volatile, and I couldn't breathe. I was in survival mode. I wouldn't just lay down for someone.

Even though I have learned to disarm my assumptions and be present with the person I am with, I still have physiological reactions that take time to slow down.

There were times when that would have messed up my whole camping experience. But now I know that I'm having a panic attack, and it's bringing back memory of fights with skinheads. I know that I need to ground myself right here, right now. All these things that I talk about doing I had to practice. Breathing, moving energy with my arms, listening to the truth in my head.

It's one thing to know what helps. Doing them in the moment is harder.

Not Allowed in The Gate

Three years later Anne asked me what I would do now if the same thing happened. I smiled as I realized that I wouldn't have the mindset that they weren't going to let me in. I used to have that thought, "Uh, they aren't going to let me in. I got to call Anne." Even before I got to the gate I would scroll through my text messages to find her house number to make sure I had her address because I would fear that if I didn't have the exact address they wouldn't let me in. My mindset was already made up that way. I fell into the worst case scenario and got worked up.

I still notice how people look at me, and I study where they are coming from. But I'm not projecting that I'm going to be a victim of a hate crime. I project that I will respect you as long as you respect me.

When I go to stores I just walk in, knowing where I'm going, and I don't feel like a bother any more. I used to say, "Oh, excuse me," and ask questions in a victim tone. Now I speak with intention. I am usually able to get what I want, and go to the cash register with no shame about myself, or about being Black, as I did in the past.

My victim stance at the gate increased the chance of being profiled. The way I am now decreases that likelihood. Profiling

> *My victim stance increased the chance of being profiled*

still exists of course, but I'm not living in a victim mindset. Being conscious of where my mind goes can help me change it, and then possibly change what triggered the feeling.

Writing Ability

Here's an example of how I let shame interfere. A couple of years ago I asked Anne if she would read what I was writing about parenting, and she was glad to. But when she sent it back she said that my writing was so poor that she couldn't give me a few pointers or an overview. She said that I needed to take college writing classes. I had capitalized a lot of words, and used no paragraph breaks. She said a few things like active and passive voice, but those are only useful for someone with basic writing ability.

A respected author and colleague was telling me that I was incompetent at something important to me.

She did agree to take my material for *Shame-Free Potty Training* and make it into a short readable book.

Now here's the weird part. She read my book description on Amazon, and was blown away by how good it was. She said it was beyond adequate, every sentence communicated a lot. And the ordering of ideas allowed the reader to flow through it.

In other words, it was the complete opposite of the other writing.

I feel differently when I write well from when I don't. When I write badly I fall into my Down Cycle distressed place, needing to journal to get it out of me and onto paper. That's different from when I wrote papers for psychology classes. Then I stepped into my adult, professional, present-day brain and did well.

But when I wrote what was flowing through my mind, the creative thinking that I had meditated my way to, it landed on the computer as incomprehensible.

Now why would that be?

Some of it may be that I couldn't read until I was in the third grade and saw myself as stupid. So I may have projected that onto the present and written as if it were true.

But I don't think so. If that were true you would think that I wouldn't be able to write at all. So why the extremes? I have to conclude that it is because of the downloaded experience of being a slave child who was taught to not let abilities show.

So I can deny my ability to communicate well by writing terribly. And by showing that to someone who I know will tell me the truth. I didn't talk to her for a time because her comments activated my shame. The shame I felt when I couldn't read when all the other kids could. But eventually I was able to see the craziness in the difference between communicating well and seeming incompetent. Then I was able to let go of the untrue version. I am competent.

Healing Shame

Developing self-esteem has helped me interact with confidence. When I have fear I go ahead anyway. I'm teaching a university level psychotherapy class on multicultural psychotherapy. They saw me as a prime candidate based on my background, my clinical skills, and my ability to talk about it. And they are right. And at the same time I have fear.

I know how to heal myself from shame. First I self-reflect. Reading

> *I know how to heal myself from shame.*

Anne's books helped me see blind spots I had avoided. Then I led groups in a treatment center on shame. Being in a group setting where everyone was able to reflect on what role shame has played in their lives and continues to play in their lives helps me normalized negative thoughts. With it in front of me I could see it for what it is. Just an obstacle. But a powerful obstacle.

I wrote *Shame-Free Potty Training* in 2020 as I recognized that not shaming my kids during toilet training had helped them succeed. This helped me see how people don't understand shame and the effect it has on kids. And how it reflects the parents' internalized shame. If a shame-free parenting style is adopted early, you are more likely to raise people who go after what they are passionate about, rather than being controlled by shame.

Chapter 6

Discomfort Being Black

Dr. DeGruy points out that we don't actually have separate races. She quotes James King in *The Biology of Race:* "There are no significant genetic variations within the human species to justify the division of 'races.'"

DeGruy says:

> Race is frequently characterized by skin color, hair texture, facial features, and so on. This assumption is simply not true. One cannot separate people into racial groups based on any set of physical characteristics....The Bushmen of southern Africa look as much Asian as they do African. Pacific Islanders have both African and Asian features. The Ainu of Japan look more European than Asian. The Sami of Scandinavia look as much like the Inuit and Yupik as they do Europeans. The Aborigines of Australia, who often look African, commonly have straight or wavy hair and are frequently blond as children.

The Complexity of Racism

All of us have been shamed just for being Black. Many of us have been stopped by police. All of us have experienced that projected feeling of being less than. The fear of it being true keeps us reliving the same negative patterns that don't serve us. This is present day racism.

Shame Passed Down From Ancestors

While the field of mental health has long known that second- and third-generation Holocaust survivors will have symptoms of being Holocaust survivors, this group is seen as innocent victims. Carrying the DNA of slave history is something else. The legacy passed down to us is being un-human stupid law breaking animals who if not controlled are to be feared.

Slaves were legally freed only a hundred and fifty years ago. And that was just the beginning of freedom. While we legally had the right to vote, it was only fifty years ago that the civil rights movement made it possible to exercise when the Voting Rights act of 1965 was passed. Our hearts and souls carry the DNA created in our ancestors from the perception of us as not people. It lives in us still.

So when we encounter a suspicious White person or police officer we have more than one kind of shame. First the current-day racism. Second, shaming from the White person across from us. Third from the definition of our ancestors.

Reducing Trauma and Shame

Addressing shame and trauma in my therapy practice has shown me how to lighten the level of it. We can recognize the physical discomfort as it appears, and have in place the skills to reduce it. It helps me to go back over the actual physical sensations of shame and fear and anxiety so I know what I want to change. And then to consciously see how changing my brain waves and heart rate can change the negative feelings.

I read slave narratives because there wasn't any other real representation of us. Hearing about people who had to fight for their education, even for the ability to read, gave me momentum. I could better understand my own privilege. This really existed, and not that long ago.

We have downloaded attitudes and emotions from those slave ancestors that we can't shed until we can see what they went through.

> *We have downloaded attitudes and emotions from slave ancestors.*

Chapter 7

African American System Trauma

I became more aware of the African American system by studying family systems and helping people understand how their identity, their communication patterns, and much of their life choices are based on the "rules" of their family. The African American system influences us in the same way.

Family System

When looking at how to heal from racism, it can help to look at how the family interacts. In my own family system I saw interactions of Black people, Mexican people, and others. As I stepped out from the some of the accepted norms of my family I got to see how there are also accepted norms of the African American system.

A family system is a group of people in a household who follow certain beliefs and behaviors. There are social rules about how people will interact with each other usually dictated by the oldest members of the family.

We fall in line with the rules. If they yell to communicate then everyone yells. It becomes normal. If the rule is being nonverbal then members won't talk. You just have to feel what's going on. If there is passive aggressive communication then the issue is never addressed, it's talked around. The norms are followed because that's what's accepted.

The younger ones follow the script. So when someone starts to communicate in a different way, like a young teen ager saying, "I don't like being talked to like this," or, "When you yell at me it makes me mad," it disrupts the family system.

A common edict of these systems is that family is first. Mine was like that. Although this can

> *"Family first" can inhibit individual identity.*

strengthen family ties and help a family survive, it can inhibit the developing of individual identity.

If someone in my family did something wrong I would take it on myself as if I did it. If someone got in an argument outside the family system it was family first. Be on your family's side. This common mindset can serve us, and it can also keep us running in patterns that no longer serve us.

I still believe in family first, but I have developed my own sense of understanding and boundaries that have come from life experience. I developed my identity when going away to college. Anyone seeing me for the first time was meeting me as an individual. I had morals and beliefs that I got from the family, but now I was integrating it. I became more of my authentic self.

When I was in the system I learned to play roles. One role was the messenger. Learning how to convey messages was one way I self-identified. I talked in a way that people could hear rather than being reactive. And now I use that in my life.

Even though I have judgments I can talk to people without judging them. I can see them as a person, an individual, rather than what they represent to me.

My dad was a police officer in an area where people didn't like police officers. I had to know that that's what my dad

> *They didn't want to be angry all the time, it's just how they knew that role.*

did for work, it wasn't who he is as a person. He was in a "police officer system." This helped me when I got older. When in trouble I could know when someone was playing the authority figure role. It wasn't that they wanted to be angry all the time, or discipline all the time, it's just how they knew that role.

Now as a father I get to decide what my role looks like, how I get to be defined. I tend to see it as a challenge, an opportunity to advance my family system.

Children are Seen as the Problem

When teens are sent to therapy, they may be starting to identify themselves as outside their family role. Their friends and peers become the most important people in their lives. They discover things they like and what they don't like, how they want to speak to people, and how they want people to speak to them. They form their own identity.

Then they go back into the family system where the communication is the same, and it creates conflict. That's why I tell the client and the parents that it's going to get worse before it gets better. Parents may think the child is being disrespectful when they are trying to express their needs.

I advise teens to take a breath, and possibly write out what they want to say. To family members. They can use the journaling practice to create bullet points to read out loud. This can help them understand how emotions and feelings play a factor in delivering a message.

If they can talk about their ideas and beliefs, and given the opportunity to debate, they may develop emotional strength so they can respectfully disagree without damaging relationships.

He could say that he stays at friends' houses because he doesn't like to hear yelling all the time. Or he doesn't like being the one who is criticized. This will relate the actual family system behavior that he wants changed.

Genogram
I ask them to draw a genogram. When you chart out each generation and how individuals may have dealt with substance abuse, physical abuse, estrangement, divorce, death, anger, and disease it becomes easier to see patterns. You may find that depression or substance abuse has been in your family for decades, but no one called it that.

Author Monica McGoldrick wrote *The Genogram Journey,* which to use her words, "Explains how drawings can reveal a

> *The Genogram Journey can reveal much about families.*

family's estrangement, alliance, divorce or suicide, exposing intergenerational patterns. It includes information on birth order, sibling rivalry, family myths and secrets, cultural differences, and couple relationships."

African American System
Family systems is studied for the purpose of family therapy. However, the bigger picture of systems includes businesses, communities, cultures, political parties, and countries. When I applied the principles of family systems to the African American system I saw how useful it is to see the rules and actions we follow as a group. It shows how breaking a system rule will disturb the system. For example, if someone goes into psychotherapy they may not talk about it because one of the rules is, "We don't do therapy." If someone works their way up in a business or profession and makes a lot of money they may be seen as "whitewashed." These people no longer fit in.

Rules of the African American System
When I understood that much of our "racism" is integrated into our very beings, I thought it would be useful to identify as many as I could think of. Instead of thinking of our choices as separate, it is powerful to see them as a grouping of requirements needed to feel like we belong. Requirements that seem to help us, and also inhibit change.

Like the teen who tells his parents that he wants them to stop yelling, once we can see the African American system we can become able to decide which components we no longer want to follow. As with the teen, making that change will be confrontive to family and friends. We can join with others so we can support each other in creating our own identity, so we can live more authentically.

We won't become White. As with the teens who get to remain family members, we get to remain Black – Black people who are extricating the harmful internalized rules of belonging.

> *We won't become White.*

One of my internalized rules is that I'm stupid. Even while allowed to be a college athlete it took me a long time to acknowledge that I'm smart. Even now I struggle with it.

Someone can call me a motherfucker and it wouldn't bother me, but if someone calls me dumb I'm ready to fight. Your allowed to be an athlete. Your allowed to be a musician. Your allowed to be an asshole or motherfucker.

Another rule is that we are not allowed to be emotional. "We don't cry about that." I want my own kids to be allowed to express their emotions, but some people will see it as disrespect. That I am allowing them to be disrespectful. But I know that it's them expressing themselves at the level they can. We can talk through it. It's okay to have these feelings.

African American System
Dr. DeGruy tells us that:

> African Americans have a unique
> socialization experience due to centuries
> of systematic and traumatic programming
> of inferiority, covering all aspects of one's
> being. In other words, from the beginning

Africans were taught they were inferior physically, emotionally, intellectually and spiritually, thus rendering them ineffectual in their own eyes and in the eyes of the society around them. At the end of slavery little changed to dispel these notions. In fact, such notions have continued to infiltrate all aspects of America life.

I will describe twenty beliefs and rules that make up this socialization. There are many more.

1. Black People are always late

It's called Black Standard Time where a Black person will be about fifteen minutes late, sometimes twenty to an hour. It's a common stereotype. It causes me to be early because even if I'm on time I still feel anxious. If a White person is late, oh, they're late. But if a Black person is late it's seen as what Black people do.

Over time when this is how Black people are seen, then it's assumed by

> *Black people are seen as late.*

us, too that, yeah, we're just going to show up late. It becomes a standard mind-set, and normal.

Lateness came from our ancestors' setbacks for getting places, including jobs. They had to get to the bus station on time. They were unable to get a cab because they're Black.

I explained to Anne how even though I seemed calm in our Zoom meeting, I had rushed to get my son awake, getting him another water bottle, then drive him to his camp, get back here, get settled, make sure I'm set up. She doesn't put this pressure on me, and when she reassured me that she was fine with a text saying "I'm late," it doesn't matter. It's pressure I put on me.

It has been passed down over generations. If slaves were late severe punishment was likely. If a slave was out of place or "not where they should be," there had to be an excuse to explain it. After freedom, discrimination could still make it difficult to predict arrival time.

When the DNA of centuries lands on us we don't realize that we have accepted the system belief that says Black people are late. Or the intense focus on making it not true.

It's like the family system where everyone yells as their standard form of communication. It makes no sense, inhibits understanding and change, but is woven into a way of life.

Many White people are habitually late but it isn't seen as part of the White system. Anne remembered a man she dated who was typically late, didn't apologize, and thought she should accept it. No one says White people are not on time.

2. Black people are on welfare. While a larger percentage of Black people are on welfare than are Whites, this is accounted for by racial inequality, including education and income levels. But over time it has become accepted as part of the African American system.

3. Beating children will give them discipline. This belief is so integrated into the system that Stacey Patton wrote *Spare the Kids: Why Whupping Children Won't Save Black America*. Beating came from slaves beaten into submission to instill fear to

obtain the desired behavior. This was passed down in the DNA, and also through the culture. Each generation observed that beaten chil-

Spare the Kids: Why whupping Children Won't Save Black America.

dren did what they were told. It is only recently established that communicating is more effective at achieving the desired outcome.

4. Not showing any emotion except anger, or no emotion at all. Having no conflict by having no feelings. You can fit in. You can belong to any group because you don't complain. People who don't feel anything will have no objections, no conflicts. You don't make a lot of noise so others are less likely to feel challenged.

5. Loud and joking.

6. Keeping a distance. This was created in slavery where they took the biggest, strongest one and made an example of him, and then then the rest fell in line. There's an old book called *The Willie Lynch Letter and the Making of a Slave,* by Willie Lynch that describes these methods. You favor one slave over the others. You give him privileges. Then the rest of the slaves will hate that one. And that one will hate them for hating him. This was to keep us in bondage, and is carried along in the Black population.

7. Public display of affection.

8. Financial wealth. If you are building wealth you are considered "whitewashed." A sellout. You're an Oreo – Black on

If you are building wealth you are considered "whitewashed."

the outside and White on the inside. This is when money is made in a legitimate way, not hustling or doing it illegally. This is changing.

I have a Black-owned business. No one can take it from me. I'm working for myself. I'm investing in myself, into my training. I learned from Black business owners. I'm learning from people who respond to my podcast interviews and Mindful Monday videos that I am countering the stereotype that says this cannot be accomplished. I had to have support to do it.

9. We mustn't be vulnerable. Being tender and open with emotions is considered a weakness. It isn't understood how

> *Being tender and open with emotions is considered a weakness*

vulnerability can be a strength. It can unite and connect people. At age thirty-five I am finally claiming it as a power instead of a weakness.

10. Black people are less intelligent than White people. The American culture has promoted that idea since slavery, and the African American system incorporated it. As a result we have not been promoted in businesses, and our presence in politics is only now evolving. It was stunning to have a Black man elected president of the United States. We can say this was postponed by voters, but our own view of what is appropriate contributed.

Difficulty beginning my business and knowing that it is appropriate to succeed and create income still speaks to me. The voice is softer but still there.

When White leaders tried to figured out how to address the inequality of education, professions, and income they came up with the idea of affirmative action to solve it. Colleges and businesses were required to accept applicants based on the percentages of Blacks to Whites.

However, this promoted the idea that the black work force was not as deserving of their positions, that they were handed a job rather than earning it.

11. We have to justify being here. When in college classes I didn't speak up because I didn't want to represent my race as being dumb. It wasn't until half way through college that I became confident that I knew what I was talking about.

When I say I teach multicultural psychology I believed that people would say, "of course they chose you because you're Black." They wouldn't believe that I could teach at a college based on my professional abilities. I also say that I teach practicum which is for all therapists as I defensively make it clear that I was chosen because of my ability.

I know that it is appropriate for me to be teaching multicultural psychology because I am well studied in it through classes and by being fascinated by it my whole life. The truth is that contrary to being seen as inferior to other teachers, I have the advantage of my experiences.

This is why experiential learning is so valuable. The Cal Poly Slogan "Learn by doing" rings in my head. I have spent much of my life learning how to facilitate difficult conversations and now I get to teach others how to hold that space.

12. Shame for being Black. We feel like a burden. I used to say "excuse me" to everybody. My wife

called me on it. She pointed out how I wouldn't ask for help, or receive what is owed to me.

The slave influence came from our ancestors being used as live-stock, not seen as people. We now have the legal rights of other races but the old role has been passed down in our DNA and the learning of each generation.

Shaming from history and continuing racism has become integrated into our view of our-

> *Shame makes me try on three sets of clothes.*

selves. I'm facing the African American shame when I try on three sets of clothes to make sure I present in an acceptable way. And when I took my White-looking children to pre-school, I was concerned about how I would be judged. When I started braiding my hair at night to get it to grow faster, I ran into a friend and as we talked I pulled out the braids so neighbors wouldn't see. I commented how a neighbor looked at me, but my friend said, "He just said hi." It's my fear of them thinking, one more Black dude fucking up the neighborhood.

13. Being a servant is an acceptable profession. We were allowed to become skilled at knowing exactly what someone else needs and providing it. We can even think beyond prescribed duties.

14. We are over sexualized. We are sexual objects, and we took this on as who we are. Being seen as forbidden fruit can make it difficult to find true intimacy. Porn commonly plays on stereotypes that all black men are sex crazed. Black men gang banging a White woman, or a Black man taking the wife of a White man.

15. We need to be afraid. *After the murder of Ahmaud Arbery, it took me a year to start running again.* This is based on reality as we know from the media and the experiences of all of us. The Innocent Black men and women being murdered. After the murder of Ahmaud Arbery, it took me a year to start running again. The shock waves of an unarmed Black Man running, and being targeted, assaulted and murdered by two White men put my whole nervous system in a fight response. This is an example of how racism has created beliefs that are then incorporated into the African American system.

16. We can be musicians. Music is in the heartbeat of the culture, and resonates through us. Singers and bands were allowed to perform, and were valued by Whites even when racism dominated. One of the reasons Jim Crow ended was because singers and artists cancelled shows in states where Jim Crow was the standard practice.

17. We don't do therapy. More than just deciding that therapy wouldn't help, the phrase, "We don't do therapy" is frequently used. While addiction treatment is becoming more common, psychotherapy is seen as not appropriate. It isn't generally understood that relief comes with letting go of automatic negative thoughts, and can help improve the quality of life. The African American system looks at mental health as an option only when there is something "wrong" or "broken." We can now look at it as a way to help advance our healing and progress.

18. Religion. We are allowed to be religious, attend services, and belong. We believe that religion is the doorway to connect with our spirituality. Religion can be beneficial because it offers morals and a basic code to live by but it can also be restrictive and harmful when dogmatic practice becomes the primary focus rather than the connection with spirituality.

19. Apologizing. We believe that apologizing for anything we may have done is natural and normal. This comes from the shame of being African Americans that has become integrated into the system. I entered my unapologetic 20s when I decided to go the polar opposite and not be sorry for anything.

20. When dating, being sure to not dominate or demand in order to avoid the perception of being needy, controlling, or aggressive.

21. We blame the racists, which sets them up to criticize and blame us more. If we blame White people then we get stuck in the victim mentality, and there's nowhere to go.

We blame White people instead of healing our wounds. And that helps perpetuate being a marginalized race. I had to heal wounds in order to be able to talk with people of other races in a dispassionate way, without my emotions triggered. Without being reactive.

> *If we blame White people we get stuck in the victim mentality.*

Now I can sit with the discomfort of knowing that what I hear in my head is remnants of past experience.

Non-polarization

When people want to argue with me, If I don't argue back, they are left hanging. They are more likely to hear what they said. I am willing to have a discussion where both parties are heard but I don't give my energy away to arguments anymore.

A friend told Anne how he and Black people get along well. He says there are no racial issues because he isn't racist. She asked how I would handle this conversation if I had been in on it.

The friend thinks there is nothing going on behind the scenes because his Black friends put on an appropriate face, smiling. I would tell him that there are actually multiple realities. I would break down how Black people have to monitor what others are feeling. If they overreact or underreact they know they will be judged. There will be microaggressions.

I would use my own experience of being with "nice" White people. I would use words that don't judge him. After talking a bit I would ask him if he would like to hear more. Even if he says no, a door might have opened into understanding that our experience is bigger than what he has known.

He may feel guilt and shame when realizing how much he didn't understand and this might prevent him from staying in the conversation. I hope that he can walk away thinking, "wow, I was able to have this conversation on race. And it felt okay." Hopefully he will see that he learned that he doesn't know everything about it.

I work hard on not judging. I will lose him or her if I become polarized. If I make it about us and them. My intention is about community and clarity. Not about I'm right you're wrong. I don't have to have someone agree with me as long as they can hear where I'm coming from. Remaining in uncomfortable openness models how I expect to be treated too.

With the friend I might say, "I respectfully disagree. I see what you are saying and I also see these other things." I would use tangible examples from my life. "I" statements. Also showing appreciation that I am hearing his experience. "Parts of what you say are real. I am just offering my lens now. A broader lens."

In one of my classes I wanted to demonstrate that my overthinking is based on reality. I had one of my White peers put on my beanie and asked the class what he looked like. The first word was Hipster with some laughter.

Then I put the beanie on myself and asked, now what do you see? The silence said it all. No one would say thug or gangster, but the point was made that we all have inherent bias.

That bias causes Black people to over-plan for safety.

I could have been a dick about it, and scoffed. When I was in Africana or Black culture study classes I could have done it to all the White people in there. But they would have been angry and walked away, and never want to have the conversation. Then we do this loop over and over again.

We have a chance to do the healing process now.

> *Now we have a chance to heal.*

I have to see how much people can hear when I describe covert racism. Sometimes they are fascinated and I keep going. Other times their eyes glaze over and I know we are done. Or maybe I shift focus to something they are able to hear.

We can acknowledge shit that's in the room that no one wants to talk about, and maybe get to our actual goal. I can look back on how I came to do that, how it became natural after a few of the Down Cycles.

When I offer an invitation I can drop my shoulders and just be where we can talk. People are usually

> *Their eyes glaze over and we are done*

willing to have the conversation. And then that trickles into my everyday life.

Covert Racism

Covert racism is the kind that isn't obvious.

When I was in college people would say to me, "I think my friend will really like you, she likes Black guys." Back then I didn't know what to call that. It would feel like a backhanded compliment. Like anyone Black will do. And it omitted the possibility that I might not be into the friend. I should just be happy she likes Black guys.

If I was dating someone who wasn't Black I would catch heat for not dating within my race, like I was being a sellout. The truth is that race was never a deciding factor of who I liked. I have always been attracted to who a person is rather than one piece of them.

The common questions in my college were, "Do you play sports?" and "What sport do you play?"

Now living in affluent areas, I'm asked if I'm a professional athlete. Just last week a sales person came to my door. When I answered in sweats he did a double take and asked, "Are you the owner of the house? Where do I recognize you from?"

My awareness of being Black is with me all the time. I won't put my hands in my pockets when I'm in a store. I keep them in front of me or behind my back or crossed. I don't want to

> *Awareness of being Black is with me all the time. I won't put my hands in my pockets in a store.*

be accused of stealing. I have a thing about not touching things in stores. My wife has no problem with it with her blond hair. In the beginning of our relationship I had to tell her that while she was comfortable, I wasn't. I couldn't walk through the store feeling like I belong and that I'm safe here. And that's hard for people to believe.

When I mentioned it in relationships they were just, "You're being paranoid." When I dated someone Black or mixed who understood then I could talk about it. It was a shared experience.

There were times when a girl would get mad and start yelling in public. For me that was not safe so I would shut down and do nothing. I've seen big Black men just stand there while someone berated them. They know if they were to react, they would be seen as a perpetrator. If I were to react I would be putting my life in danger. Learning that other black men dealt with this fear was an incentive to continue to find ways to help heal it.

Meditation Helps

Meditation helped with the anger I didn't know what to do with. It took me years to figure out how to flip those switches and subdue it. I feel crazy at times because I have a lot going through my mind that others don't see. I'm afraid if I articulate it I would look crazy. But when I read about the people who stood up and took the brunt of the civil rights movements I gained more of a sense of power. I saw there has been change.

Diagnosis Paranoid Schizophrenia

In my internship in graduate school I worked with people with paranoid schizophrenia. When working with them on a daily basis I started to see past the label. I could actually hear the story of how they got to that point. I was able to see how enough trauma, misunderstanding, lack of safety and lack of rest could truly fracture the mind.

It triggered my fear that if I were diagnosed it would take away the validity of what I say. It hurt when people told me I was crazy because my viewpoint was different. If I have a diagnosis then they can say, "oh, yes, you are crazy."

Then nothing I say is valid. I'd be easily dismissed.

Thoughts in my mind can get loud and I can be afraid of them. I don't want someone to ask if I hear voices because if I say yes, then, okay, here's the stamp on your head that you're crazy. I asked a doctor if he heard voices in his head when he was thinking about things, and he said, "No," in such a way that I decided that I shouldn't talk about it.

When I was younger I didn't know how to describe it. Because of the role of religion I thought it was God talking to me. I later learned that it is my consciousness speaking. My higher self. I hear clients describe it too.

After hearing people acknowledge their crazy-seeming thoughts, I could believe that I'm not crazy. I get to explore these thoughts that have upset me in the past. This is one reason why journaling is so important. I could see the intensity and urgency in my thoughts, which helped me slow it down.

Graduate School, a Studio Apartment, an Emotional Break

I lived in a studio apartment on very little money while working on my Master's degree in psychology and putting in long hours at the mental health clinic. I had sixteen-hour shifts, little sleep, and was sometimes in charge of thirteen severely mentally ill clients by myself. The stress brought me to the bottom of my Cycle. One day stood out as especially difficult.

I circled around my apartment experiencing my craziness. I had been self-medicating with alcohol and drugs. I was diagnosing people's mental illness at the clinic. And I was going to classes in my Master's program.

I fell into a very dark place and wondered how I could navigate myself back. Even going to therapy didn't feel like a good idea because I didn't expect my craziness to be understood. Maybe even diagnosed the way I was diagnosing others.

Alone in my studio, as each thought overlapped the others, I didn't know what to do next. But I knew that I needed to do something. I was agitated. And lost. I had the TV and music on as I tried to distract myself. I hadn't said a word in two days. I hadn't talked with anyone who is technically sane in three to four days.

If I spoke I expected to be perceived as scary, paranoid, or just plain crazy. I wasn't able to be who I am. It felt unsafe to be vulnerable. I had to find a route out of this. I couldn't depend on anyone else to pull me out.

So what was my escape route?

I was trying to find a playbook to explain. What would the healing properties be? Psychedelics helped with depression because they let me see reality in a different way. But if I were to tell somebody, I believed they would say "this is why you are crazy." I feared I would be dismissed as a drug addict. And now ten years later research is showing evidence that it can help relieve trauma and depression.

I became able to go back and forth between that crazy state and leaving it with meditation and exercise. I put down pillars to identify where I was each time. In my clinic work I talked with people who were in that extreme state, but they were stuck in it. They were unable to come back. They were too scared to try to come back. When I spoke with them I could see that the person was still there, but was lost.

That experience showed me how fragile the mind can be if overworked. I stopped believing the labels, "paranoid" and "insane," that kept me from being vulnerable.

As I described this to Anne, I wondered if I should put it in the book. But now when working with therapy students I see how much we all have to face. After witnessing how many have broken down during the isolation of the pandemic, the fear of discussing fears showed me that I need to tell my experience. We all need to know that these extreme states do not need to be forever. They can be momentary if we don't avoid them.

When I was working sixteen hour shifts and not sleeping I had my first suicide client. I was band-aiding so many things that I couldn't protect myself. I lived in social isolation. I learned to numb. I think many people get to that point but don't recognize it.

Even in Santa Barbara on the ocean I couldn't see beauty. Not until later.

A lot of people create that crazy cocktail themselves. Their survival mode is so thick they can't see that there is also beauty. And that transformation is possible. So that's why I'm letting you see my experience.

My Own "Karen" Woman

I was working out with callisthenic pull up bars in a park in what was to become my new neighborhood when a White woman walked up and took her dogs off leash. It's in a cul de sac so there was no place to walk away. I was the only Black person. I usually cover my tattoos and dress in ways to be not threatening.

With my shirt off my tattoos showed when she walked toward me. She was approaching faster than I expected, and I quickly put my shirt back on. The dogs were coming my way too. My adrenalin was pumping because my conditioning made

me believe a racist wom-
an was coming toward
me. Like she had a pre-

> *People lock the door
> when I walk by.*

conceived notion of who I am. I'm use to people
locking the door when I walk by and not making
eye contact.

I pleaded in my mind for her to stay away. Please
stay over there. I don't want to have to work to
make you feel safe. That's usually what I feel, that
I have to go out of my way to make sure they feel
safe so I feel safe. I was resentful. They should
make me feel safe. This is my space now.

Looking back I can see how much internal monologue I listened to, compared to seeing what was
actually going on. And I made up her internal
monologue, something like, "I don't know this
guy, I don't know who he is." Of course I couldn't
see that I was making it up.

I was reacting to her. And she could very well
react to my reaction to her. Around and around.

My mind went to the Karen woman situation in
the 2020's where the Black man in Central Park
recorded the woman on his cell phone. I wondered if I should record this for my defense as
I've had people call the cops just because of walking by their house. Or thinking I stole something.
In that moment I went back to many past experiences.

This wasn't thought out, it was just felt. Do I
record or not?

I was able to decide to do this differently than I
had in the past. Back then I might show off my
tattoos or my physique in an aggressive way. Be-

ing six foot and 180 pounds, others react. I could feel safer by being more aggressive. In high school and college it was common to meet aggression with more aggression.

Doing it Differently This Time

But in that moment I went to my breath. My breathing exercises. Noticing how my body was tightening up, my muscles getting in that fight-flight-freeze response, I started to do Tai Chi. I put my hands above my head and focused into the electromagnetic energy throughout my body. Then I could notice what was happening. I moved up my energy centers starting with number one at my tail bone for grounding. Then on up to my solar plexus and trying to stay open in my heart space.

I drew on what I learned from the book, *How the Body Keeps the Score: Brain, Mind and Body in the Healing of Trauma*. I had read about my own experiences with meditation and yoga helping to reduce and heal from trauma.

> *Meditation and yoga in* How the Body Keeps the Score: Brain, Mind and Body in the Healing of Trauma.

I focused on breathing in and breathing out. Fast on the inhale, slow on the out. Paying attention to it. I knew this would calm my cardiovascular system. I made sure I didn't hyperventilate. As I expanded my body I could feel energy in my hands, so I rubbed them together and held them over my body to slow my nervous system down.

I'm a beginner in Tai Chi and Chi Gung, but it didn't take much to have an effect. I didn't have to be an expert to move energy in a way that let me calm my body and become more conscious.

She walked up and said, "Hi. What are you doing?"

My internal state said she was threatening, but she wasn't. Inside I had pleaded, please stay away, please stay over there. But I had calmed myself and was able to see that if she had a good experience with just one Black person it might change her perception. I even thought this at the time.

When I was at Cal Poly I was usually the only Black person in my classes. The few times there were others was usually because we decided to take them together. So as a psychology student I was the only one to speak for my culture. I had to articulate so I didn't scare people or so they could be open to conversations. Even when writing for classes I would throw in big words to prove that I wasn't just an angry Black person screaming and yelling. I wanted to show that there is evidence behind what I was saying.

We started talking. I explained how I'm a therapist trained in trauma and I was reducing stress. I gave a little information about the brain and the breath and how it's possible to manage anxiety. She took it all in. Then she talked about being an airline server and how she had to deal with people on planes with aggressive attitudes and it's all about how you talk with them.

We had a good conversation.

This woman was obviously safe to be around, yet my programing forced me to use my calming methods anyway. A White woman walking toward me while taking her dogs off leash triggered a trauma response.

> *A White woman walking toward me while taking her dogs off leash triggered a trauma response.*

I noticed her change because of our non-threatening interaction. As she saw me deliberately breathing and raising my hands over my head in a ritual style, her shoulders relaxed. As she relaxed, her voice changed. And she began imitating my movements. We breathed together and moved our arms in the same manner. It became pleasant to relate.

She said it was great speaking with me, hoped I had a good day, and we went our separate ways.

Discomfort Being Black

I expected my children to have dark skin but neither does, so when I took them to nursery school it looked like a Black man dropping off White kids. Now what's wrong with that? It could be adoption, as I had always asked been when I was with my mother or my step parents. Or they could have thought I was a care giver. But in my racist thinking I believed that it wasn't acceptable. I expected to be judged. So I never went in sweats just out of bed in the morning. I wore professional work clothes.

I was so insecure that I didn't look at anybody at the school. I didn't want to see the criticism. I wanted to just get there and go. So I cut myself off from everyone's energy. I wouldn't stick around even though my son wanted me to stay and play with the kids.

While I want to think that this was uncalled for, it can still go on. A friend who is married to a White woman was in Scotland with three of their young White grandchildren when he was almost attacked for holding one on his shoulders. They threatened him. If I had been there with my own children I would have received the same threats.

Even though I have wiring to be afraid of racist judgment I had lessor forms because of my grandparents being in the military. Military racism is different because they are put together to win. A relationship is built within the system. When obstacles are overcome together it creates a bond that allows those involved to let go of made up difference such as race. You win together. This is not to say there isn't systemic racism, but the difference is that mindset of working together transfers to the next generation. It is witnessed as a possibility. You're in a melting pot. The parents see themselves as Americans, fighting for our country. Together.

I'm in a melting pot. I have White relatives, Black relatives, Mexican relatives, and many people in my family are mixed.

But even though I came from the least constrictive kind of racism, still, when walking into a White nursery school as a Black man with White children, I froze

When walking into a White nursery school as a Black man with White children, I froze.

Those of you who grow up in an all-Black community and all you know of White people is what you see on TV and sometimes the police, you have to reprogram all these pieces of how you see your reality. This is true for White people who grew up in an all-White community, too. Getting away from racism means both have to re-program their view of life. Being non-racist is a lot more than the feeling of acceptance. It requires exposure to others and empathizing with their experience.

And even though I had it easier than most, it has been hard. Acknowledging my privilege let me drop the shame that keeps me form empathizing with others. I don't need to have gone through what others have to be able to connect with a person who is suffering. If anything, it can invoke my curiosity.

As an athlete in college I hung out with other athletes, not just Black. I was in a fraternity that was predominantly White. My White roommate was my best friend. Having immersed myself in White communities I can understand when disconnect is happening. I can see the bigger picture of what's going on and what is needed. I can see the questions within the big picture of systemic racism.

And still I tensed up when approached by a White woman with dogs. And in a nursery school with White children and parents.

Section II

Healing Myself

Chapter 8

Journaling

In the middle of my senior year in high school I was a two post varsity athlete getting ready for my third trip to State for the 110 high hurdles. I had scholarship offers to California and Ivy League schools for running track. I had friends all over the country. I had a job at a hotel, a car, and freedom.

And I was incredibly angry. I was anxious all the time. I was depressed. Whenever I tried to talk to family or friends, I felt guilty for saying that I felt the way I did, and before I could finish I would usually say, "Never mind." I would be told, "How can you feel depressed, you have everything! You have friends, you are athletic. What do you have to be depressed about?" My hygiene became really bad. I didn't want to brush my teeth or wash my face. It was chalked up to being a "teenage boy."

These waves of depression would continue through my early twenties. I didn't know that

> Depression doesn't exist for Black people.

the feeling was depression, as depression didn't exist for Black people.

I figured I was lonely, or that I needed to be in a relationship to be complete. I would self-medicate with drugs and alcohol to numb the hole I felt. I would get into fist fights just so I could feel something different. I wanted to be punched in the face because then I could fight back. Fight mode felt comfortable because I wouldn't feel anxious or depressed.

I had been self-numbing for so long it got to the point that the only time I was feeling good was when I was under the influence, having sex, or working out. I had gotten so good at numbing emotional pain that I lost sight of my emotions. Most people who knew me knew I could be the life of the party, but they didn't know what was going on in my head and what it was like when I went home alone. The only people that got a glimpse of what I was going through emotionally were my roommates and maybe a few girlfriends that had gotten to know more sides of me.

Journaling was Self-Care

The only place I was comfortable sharing my thoughts was in my Journal. I wouldn't write every day, but when I did I would let everything out. I wouldn't judge my thoughts. I would be able to put them on the page and then close the book and let them go.

When I had flashbacks of past traumas I would write them down, even when not knowing what it was, but still recording.

When I was twenty-five I started looking back at what I had written. I noticed patterns. I would see that during certain times of the year I would be more down, very pessimistic and dark. Not seeing anything good. All my entries would be negative. This would be after breakups or not accomplishing a goal.

And then there would be times when I was manic. I was looking through a completely different lens. I had all these ideas and aspirations. My handwriting was different. I would think of writing books, or how I would become a therapist.

This pattern showed up all through my writing, although I didn't understand why at the time. I was able to be aware of when my highs and lows would change. I knew that in October through December I would have lower energy. I would self-medicate more than usual.

In February through June I would have an excess of energy. I would get a lot done as long as I planned beforehand. I was able to track when I was better at making plans and when I was better at executing them.

If I didn't have all this written down my memory would have lied to me. I would have been

> *I claimed being curious as a way of life.*

able to continue generalizing what the problem was and it would have always been someone else's fault. I would have stayed the victim, or continued trying to not be the victim. I was able to validate my experience and empathize with that old self. I was able to learn from those experiences rather than see them as a waste of time or a "failure." I claimed being curious as a way of life.

At last I was able to take accountability for my actions and how I had contributed to my own problems. I could look from my new lens and see what aspects of the situation I wasn't willing to examine back then. I was able to change my life but not because someone else told me I needed to, and not because I felt guilt for who I was being. I was able to change because I was tired of seeing the same cycle play out. I wanted change. I was motivated to change. I had evidence of how and why I kept getting the same results. I could almost time it within a two month window. But first I had to be curious. The opposite of giving in to the status quo.

> *I accepted my need to grow and change*

And that was how I started developing Cycle Theory as my model for healing trauma. As I developed the process, I became able to track how I was perceiving things and how I interacted.

Discipline

When I started understanding discipline, I became able to do things because I knew it was right for me. So instead of thinking that something like meditation wasn't important, and not doing it, I did it anyway. Discipline. So when I feel challenged by what's going on in the country or my family, I know I need to be stricter with self-care. I need to meditate a little more, I need to do my routines.

I liked understanding the routines of the Muslim culture. How they pray at the same times every day. Not that I'm Muslim, just that I saw what it did for them that I could adopt. I take from Christianity, Hinduism, and Buddhism, too. I see how specific practices can be relied on to provide order when life feels chaotic. And to keep it from feeling that way. This is how I can make sense of things, how I can have my calm moment in contemplative practices. In prayer. In meditation.

Mentors

In my early twenties I started finding people who could help. Mentors. People who could show me how to walk in different ways. Being able to hear how Black business people navigated systemic racism. That it's possible. Having the perspective that this is attainable changed my perspective.

I had professors like Dr. Ryujin and Dr. Teramoto-Padrotti who helped me advocate for myself and modeled walking their own journey as members of the AAPI (Asian American Pacific Islander) community. Their ability to empathize with students from all walks of life and hold space for some of the toughest conversations while not shaming has been key to my ability as a professor.

If I believe it's impossible to heal from systemic racism then I'm just going to be angry and bitter for

> *I'm not going to be angry and bitter for the rest of my life*

the rest of my life. I see how it effects people. But if I know that I can be a conduit of change and growth, it's empowering. It makes it easier for me to get up in the morning knowing that yes, I'm going to have difficulties. It's just a hurdle. It's just something I'm going to step over.

When I'm exhausted it's harder to get in that mindset. When I'm aware that I'm exhausted I give myself a little more grace. I'm not going to put myself in situations where I'm going to fail. At the time of writing this I'm in the middle of a lot and it's stressful. So much going on in the world. I like to think I'm out of it, above it, but my thought process is hijacked by it. That means I need to put in more self-care. Meditate more. Be stricter in my discipline. That's helping me maintain a sense of calm when putting this information in writing.

As I became stronger through discipline, including self-care, I was changed. I started to see how people approached me. People were no longer sucking away at my power, taking from me. My shoulders stopped rolling forward. People commented on my strong aura. Several thought I was taller by an inch or two. This is because I could walk into a room and carry myself. I wanted to be able to do that when I was sixteen, eighteen, and twenty-one. As I started to discipline myself in my practices even more, I found tribes to be with. Now I could find mentors such as Anne and professors who I could connect with. To have intellectual conversations that bypassed race. That was something I could actually feel.

When I started thinking that everyone was looking at me because I'm Black, my shoulders would clench. My shame made me think there's something wrong with being Black when there isn't. It was different when I got to where I could have a conversation with a White person and believe that they weren't just seeing me as Black.

Now I usually feel confident in places where there are no other Black people. And I know that others will be able to get to that point. The switch has to be turned. To do that we have to lean into the discomfort of it.

> *I lean into discomfort.*

I've become comfortable being uncomfortable.

When Anne and I became friends my experience of being Black included noticing that she was an older White woman, and so I took longer to trust that she cared for me. But I could also sense that she did, and that it was real and good. I could feel it.

But later when she critiqued my early writing, I went into shame. I didn't talk with her for a time. I thought I was dumb, stupid. My mind said, "You're never going to succeed." It took time to notice this and then to have the words to articulate it. To see what was going on in my mind.

Now while this didn't have to do with my color, my feeling of being

> *I tried to prove I wasn't less-than*

less-than did. I spent years trying to prove that I wasn't less-than. I had to get in a fight, or wear a big chain, or talk in a certain way. I had to be the best athlete. I couldn't be mediocre.

I love playing basketball but I didn't play in high school because I didn't want to hear how a White dude crossed me up, or references to how I should be good because of being Black. When I was a track athlete, I heard statements like, you're Black, of course you're fast. I didn't start playing basketball again until my teammate at Cal Poly would force me to play with him after practice. Then I actually enjoyed it.

I resisted so many stereotypes. I avoided things I loved to avoid other's beliefs.

Chapter 9

Yoga

When I was in high school my friend's mom asked me if I wanted to go to yoga class because stretching might help with my running. So I went to a few classes, and I was amazed. I could slow myself down. The lights were dim so no one was looking at me. Everyone concentrated on themselves. To be able to lie in the dead pose, and just be there. Being awake but not doing anything. I didn't know that was meditation. I thought, I'm just doing yoga.

My coach in college had us do yoga, too, but he didn't call it that. He had us focus on ourselves. I noticed my breathing, how I would breathe in, and when exhaling I would go farther into the posture. It relieved these things I was hanging on to.

When in grad school in Santa Barbara living on nothing I couldn't afford a gym membership but I could afford a yoga membership. So between classes and working at the mental health facility I would go to yoga. No one described it as meditation.

But again there was this meditative thing happening. No one had to describe it to me. In my first grad school class a teacher who did movement therapy and dance therapy had us meditate for fifteen minutes before each class. We would just focus on our breathing and notice what was going on as she guided us. It was the most relieving thing I had experienced. I knew nothing about guided meditation, but I felt centered. My mind was fully in my body for the first time.

> *My mind was fully in my body*

I was conscious of everything going on but I wasn't reactive to it. This was a first. I hadn't been able to have people behind me before, I had to have my back against the wall and be able to see everything. Now my jaw relaxed, my body relaxed, and I could be in a room full of people.

So I started to do this for five to ten minutes. Living in Santa Barbara I could run to the beach, so that became my routine. Run to the beach with my books and meditate. I committed to going to the beach more than once a week and entering this calm experience. I watched the waves and did my breathing and got into a state of meditation.

This was in contrast to my clinical work where people were screaming all hours of the night. The people there had had a lot of trauma. Some were coming out of locked facilities and others were facing going in.

I could work sixteen-hour shifts, see my future wife, go to classes, study, and write papers. I was in better shape doing all of that then when I was training as an undergraduate track athlete. Everything was in sync.

Before I set out to change I blamed others for how I was feeling. But now when I wasn't relating with others I had to look at myself. What was I doing?

My old way was to hit the red button and turn everything off. Dissociate, disconnect. Turn off the emotion. Now I'm embracing it from a state of curiosity rather than judgment and panic.

I walked through it. I could be by myself for longer periods of time. I could look at the transformation, and validate it instead of thinking I was just in a wormhole and wouldn't make it out.

Chapter 10

Cycle Theory and Practice

I worked at taking Cycle Theory from theory to practice. You know how you feel great at times, and then drop down into a less enjoyable experience? I discovered that accepting these shifts as normal makes life flow along more easily. If we know that we will have the down experiences it makes it easier to accept them. If we think we have to be up and feeling great all the time we are set up for self-criticism when shifting to the natural down experience.

Accepting Cycles helps life flow

It helps me to realize that our lives are impacted by changes. Cycles of change. Imagine waves moving forward and back. We go through seasonal cycles, lunar cycles, weekly cycles. We attach meaning to them. How Monday compares with Friday. What spring feels like as opposed to winter. Our energy levels change.

We naturally shift up when things are going well or possibly because of the time of day or month or year. When in a healing process we will go up when changing for the better, and then automatically drop into the Down Cycle.

We lose sight of these Cycles because our work life, school life, and interpersonal relationships influence our experience. If we have had a traumatic event happen during a particular time, say around Christmas, it may have a negative impact on how we feel in December. Without processing the trauma we may think that December sucks without getting to the cause. I found that journaling helped me see the times of year, and also what happened during my change periods. Once I could see then I could accept and make use of the down periods as well as the ups.

When we understand our Cycles we can use self-care to give ourselves needed emotional and physical nurturing. I rest more, sit outside, go to the beach, and play with my kids. I make tasty food and ask my wife for special care. Associating positive gentle self-care helps me accept the downs and it makes them less down.

When we don't understand the natural nature of the down Cycle we criticize it, often using ways it avoid feeling it such as drinking or getting busy. We think that we must return to normal instead of allowing ourselves to process life experiences. Understanding how your Cycles work allows you to be prepared for even extreme states – manic when up and depressed when down.

Cycling Up and Down

As I worked on this book I discovered how I Cycled up and down. Sometimes I had to just sit, and be in it. Habits that weren't serving me showed up. One is telling myself to get busy, use this time. I thought I was being productive but I was just distracting myself.

I had to reveal my history to Anne in a vulnerable way, which brought up all kinds of discomfort. Sometimes it triggered me for a day or more into the Down Cycle. And then I talked about that in our next meeting.

We talked about slave history. I had slave ancestors, of course, along with other ethnicities. Anne's

> *We are Black people and White people healing*

great grandmother had been married to a slave owner. She sought out history of that family. Here we are, the offspring of slaves and slave owners working together on a book about healing from the effects of slavery. Black people and White people healing the effects.

We spent our meetings talking about the material for this book, and walking through my transformation. A couple of months after my birthday I shifted into the Up Cycle and became committed to this project. I had relieved enough of my fears of being successful and my fears of failing that I could imagine the book in my hand, ready to give out in a few more months. We shifted from the processing mode to focus on the project itself. I had to have an acceptance and validation of my experience before moving forward.

Journaling
Sometimes I just needed to write things out. To express them. And then I discovered that it was a way to slow down my nervous system. I could be conscious of my state of mind instead of being reactive, getting caught in emotions.

I became able to start tracking my Cycles. Throughout the years I would notice that during certain months I was more emotionally reactive than in other months. I was in the Down Cycle.

At these times I needed to get up at five in the morning to work out, and then get main tasks done because by noon my mind would be gone.

> *The inner healer starts to take shape.*

Sometimes I journal about how well things are going, how I am handling everything and the family is strong. When I have bad days I record that I am frustrated and irritable. I can't express it to anyone, but I can put it in writing. Then I can validate my experience at a later time. The inner healer takes shape.

There are the times when I have to write down the tasks I have in front of me so I don't forget them. Knowing I will do them in the morning relieves the stress. I cross them out as I complete them. Then I write down what I have done because when I feel good about it, I am reinforcing the feeling. When I don't get them done I practice feeling okay about being imperfect. I'm still working on that one.

I remember that it's my body and my consciousness telling me something. I ask myself, what are my options for changing? Maybe I can make a small change. Maybe go to sleep a little earlier this month. Maybe take it easy on my workouts. Maybe I'm going to meditate a little more so my physical body doesn't get exhausted.

When a relationship ended I would write about it. I would learn from it so it didn't throw me off my course. I didn't feel like I lost time.

During one breakup, a test was coming up, and at the same time I was stressed about a job I was trying to get. So of course I was exhausted. Of course I was more irritable. I could see that it was more than me being a chaotic mess. That understanding helped me not go out to the bars every weekend. I went to the beach instead. I would exercise because it says in my journal that when I exercise I feel more grounded and present.

> *I learn what I need to do next from journal writing.*

I learned from my writing. It wasn't someone else saying, "You need to do this, L.J. You need to do that. This is what you should do to be an adult."

No. Instead, I don't like being hung over at work, and I wrote about it. Seeing what I wrote I thought, maybe I need to change that. It gave me a sense of accountability. And I latched onto understanding the Cycle. The Up Cycle is pleasant, I enjoy my life and walk comfortably. And then the Down Cycle will consistently appear. I will struggle, and need to use my supportive self-care to feel better. I watch it, learn about it, and grow from it. And I remember that I will soon Cycle Up.

I Have a Gift

Putting all my experiences together I know that I can walk into a hostile environment and be okay. I know I can smooth out places that don't look like they can be. I know I won't be harmed. This is a special ability that came from more than experiences. I came into life with an ability that I then developed. It's a spiritual capacity that I can't get my hands on to talk about. I just found myself doing it.

I fear what will happen if I am more public with my abilities to think and communicate. After all,

Martin Luther King, Malcom X, and others were assassinated for speaking out. When choosing pictures of Black people to put on the walls of my office I chose those who weren't killed because of their public appearances. I have Barack Obama on my wall, I have Jim Brown. Jesse Owens. I put people who remained who they were and didn't compromise themselves, and who continued to live.

I don't know how much of that is just being in a Down Cycle place of fear. Perhaps it's to remind myself that doing what I am doing doesn't mean having to be a martyr.

Seeking to Understand Systemic Racism

Growing up around my grandparents I heard about what it was like in the day, what I wasn't taught in school. I wanted to know the truth. It felt good to make educators hear reports on slave narratives. I confronted them with truth about Black history.

I was into Malcom X in high school. I learned about the Black Panthers. I learned about Buffalo Soldiers in the Civil War on the side of the North. They were some of the strongest soldiers with the best records. I wanted to know why this wasn't taught in school.

When I brought it up to my grandfather, who's a military veteran, he helped me learn more about my culture, and understand where I was coming from. It's a broken historical record.

Luckily my natural curiosity got me to keep reading, and I saw how little the people who haven't done that reading know.

One of the first books was *Twelve Years a Slave* about the experiences of a free Black man who was kidnapped and sold into slavery. It was made into a movie. I was horrified to learn that the typical experience of being a slave was being overworked and regularly whipped. He was given positions of authority over slaves, and had to whip them. If he didn't then he would be whipped.

Now I know that the ancestral downloading of that is why the book, *Spare the Kids: Why Whupping Children Won't Save Black America* by Patton is necessary. Over generations Black America took on the brainwashed belief that whipping causes desirable behavior.

I suffered through that reading, shocked to learn how my very ancestors had been treated.

Another book was about a slave who bought his freedom, but I don't remember the name. He married a White woman who taught him to read as it had been illegal for a slave to learn. It was also illegal for them to be married because they were biracial, which helped me see how some laws applied directly to my existence. Knowing that my parents' marriage would have been illegal in some states and that my existence as a Blaxican (Black Mexican) was looked down on caused me pain and self-doubt.

Systemic racism that can come from within our African American system can be as brutalizing as that of White racism.

> *The internalized systemic racism can be as brutalizing as White racism*

Racism is learned and passed down. Once it is

normalized laws and beliefs continue until confronted. It took a while to make sense of it. When
I got to high school it sank in and I became angry
because I didn't have a way to disrupt and change
this system.

Chapter 11
Religion and Spirituality

I was raised Christian and spent a lot of time in church when my parents were splitting up. Over time I explored other religions and realized that they are basically saying the same things. I went to a Christian non-denomination church and a Catholic school which showed me the difference between the sects of the same religion.

Luckily my high school religion teachers were open minded so I was into religion classes because my teachers actually wanted to talk. When I questioned the religion they responded. It wasn't out of disrespect, it was curiosity. I was rewarded in those classes because they liked that I would engage with them.

When I was in high school I had a class on world religion. I was like, okay, in church we were told about the Iraq war

> *Why would religions forsake those in the other religion?*

and we were supposed to seek revenge and cause harm after 911. But what about the Muslim kid I imagined before? Why would both of our religions forsake those in the other religion as a good person? I thought about how he could possibly be a better human being than I was being. This is important. I was imagining a person rather than a label of something that isn't human.

When I saw them as humans it made it impossible to think of harming him.

This led me on a study of spirituality. I paid attention to how I felt when praying or singing in worship. How good it felt. But I also saw how much of that was overshadowed by the guilt and shame that was used for control. I started feeling manipulated so I didn't want to be in a church where we were taught that this is the only way to connect to the higher power.

English and Spanish and other languages were spoken where I grew up so religions seemed like just different languages. They are all trying to describe a way of being in this world.

When Muslims pray to Allah, they have a whole ceremony. The prayers are like a song. And the bowing down is like in the Christian church. I saw these similarities. Buddhists use beads to help meditate, like the Catholic rosary. Instead I try to be in the present moment, letting go. Being curious. Noticing the experience. Noticing shame and letting it go.

Spiritual practices get added onto, and become dogmatic. We put people in boxes. The spirituality can lose the healing quality.

My dad is a history buff and I learned a lot from him. I would go to church with my mom, come home and hang out with my dad, and we would talk about the history of what I learned that day. So I got a broad look that made spirituality and religion interesting to me. Now I have the freedom to walk away from dogma.

Chapter 12

Self-Care

"Oh, no, I'm depressed. How long is it going to last?" That's the old perception. Now I can ask myself, what was the onset? And what are my self-care tools? I wrote them all down so I could more easily engage in nurturing self-care when needed. And then I could see when it was time to get to work on the constructive kind.

Nurturing Self-Care

These are the choices that feel good in the moment. It can be a special food, or a conversation with someone you enjoy. Going to a movie, watching Netflix, sitting outside. A hot bath. Taking a nap. It does not require any work. However, if I do too much of this I can become apathetic. There isn't much growth in this type of self-care.

Constructive Self-Care

This self-care takes work. It may not feel good in the moment, but is improving yourself or your life in ways you value. It could be learning a language or working out or taking classes, or cleaning the house or garage or doing yard work. I work on keeping a balance between the two, often starting with the nurturing kind and then when feeling better, shifting to the constructive ones.

Too Much Nurturing Self-Care.
When I graduated college I had finished four years of competing at the D1 Level as a 110 High Hurdler. The amount of training and scheduling is mind-numbing to think about now. For the first time since I was ten I wasn't training for the next season in a sport. No coaches checking in on me, no 6 am weight training, no heating my legs before practice and icing after. I literally got four to six hours out of my day back.

I now had time for self-care, but my nurturing self-care consisted of movies partying, and gaming. I would play video games, then watch some movies, then go out to party, and repeat the cycle over and over.

After a month or so I felt depleted and apathetic. I hadn't accomplished anything. I was just doing things that felt good in the moment. There were no lasting positive feelings. There was no progress or growth.

I had lost the balance of "work hard play hard." Work had been school and sports. They were my constructive self-cares.

But then I kept playing and stopped working.

Running every day for eight years helped release neurotic energy. Exercise was my first constructive self-care. It was easy to mark progress and gains. Working out had also become nurturing self-care. I hadn't realized this because I still thought of it as a responsibility rather than a way to de-stress. Eventually I started to add more constructive self-care as my energy levels started to rise.

Too Much Constructive Self-Care

Meditation was one of the most difficult things for me to learn. Sitting still was impossible. My thoughts were heavy and my body had to move. So walking meditation and yoga introduced me to sitting meditation. I was so hyper-focused on the future or lamenting my past that being present was painful. As my clarity, memory, and awareness improved, though, I started to meditate more. Noticing how I became less reactive reinforced the practice.

But then I took it to an extreme. I was constantly working on self-healing. I wanted to analyze and assess everything. I was constantly breaking down my ego and reconstructing. This was a powerful practice, but I did too much too fast and ended up with no real defenses. I was emotionally raw and depleted and I didn't have roots to keep me grounded. This caused me to stay in a Down Cycle longer, the way that over exercising and pulling muscles makes recovery time longer.

A second example is my studies. I love psychology. The study of why people do what they do fascinates me. When I was in grad school I took nine hours of class, worked forty hours a week in a residential mental health program, and saw individual clients. I was living and breathing psychology. I was learning how to be a better clinician. The stories and traumas I heard were on top of overanalyzing my personal experience and were helping me grow as a clinician at a fast pace.

Three things were causing me even more distress. I over-empathized with my clients' pain, feeling it along with them. I was hypervigilant, as usual. And, worst of all, believed that I wasn't a good enough therapist. I was on, but I wasn't giving myself the nurturing selfcare I needed.

Compassion fatigue and resentment was the result of too much constructive self-care. I was irritable toward people who loved me. I was annoyed with my clients and their seeming lack of understanding of how much I was putting into our sessions. I had to drop back and take better care of myself to let that go.

Constructive self-care can become the nurturing form. Mediation for me is now nurturing. When I make time to meditate it feels good in the moment. If you are playing an instrument it starts as a struggle, then through that struggle you might find a state of flow, and enjoyment. Self-care can create growth.

Shadow Side

As a therapist I believe in paying attention to the positives. The hope. The gratitude. But I also acknowledge there has to be the other side too. I believe that many clinicians focus too much on the positive. Our clients need us to be able to go to the shadow side with them so they can find ways to accept their full self, and not just label it as good or bad.

> *Therapists need to go to the shadow side with clients*

If I can just talk about it then I can see what it is. When I can talk about my shadow side, that darkness, I know there will be relief. I can know there is no scary monster in the shadows.

When I grind my teeth it's a sign that I'm stressed out. I wake up tired and my jaw hurts. Once I can be curious about it, I ask myself how I can be in a place that isn't fear based. I go back to my tools to ground myself. I have to practice over and over because I flow in and out of this state. The tools I use may be different based on where I am at in the journey.

The Full Catastrophe of Living

I'm using the book, *The Full Catastrophe of Living* by Jon Kabat-Zinn in my class for psychology students. It helped me get into mindfulness and has tools and techniques to help us get through the day. He created what he calls mindful-based stress reduction (MBSR). People go to his center for physical pain, migraines, depression, anxiety, trauma, and more. They have a program on line which you can do for free.

> The Full Catastrophe of Living *has mindfulness techniques.*

I have read this book many times over many years, including at three in the morning with my baby daughter. He described what he did with his fussy baby, and how he would meditate to her breathing. And then use his own breath to sooth her. While using this technique I found that instead of seeing the situation as a hassle, it became a relaxing bonding time between my daughter and me.

The Practice of Cycle Theory

When I became emotionally rigid I used to feel shameful, but now I accept it. It's part of who I am. If I can stay away from judging I can be curious about why this is coming up. Then I'm likely to move forward to a solution.

When I'm on the top of the Cycle I feel hyper, full of energy. When I'm at the bottom of the Cycle I have a hard time getting things done. It looks like depression, isolation, wanting to get away from everybody. I feel lethargic. I don't relate it to all that energy I was putting out in the hyper phase, where I exhausted myself.

I don't judge myself any more. I just know that this is where I'm at. And I use nurturing self-care. I will journal about things I want to get done. One time it was about starting my practice. I didn't know how to get a business license, I couldn't think of a name, I didn't know how to start a website, I didn't know how to market. These things were overwhelming as I was hitting my down slope.

It was like moving through quicksand. Nothing was getting done. I was making no progress, and I kept getting deeper and deeper in that Down Cycle.

As I journaled I named the tasks I wanted to do. And I was reading the book, *Breaking the Habit of Being Yourself: How to Lose Your Mind and Create a New One,* by Dr. Joe Dispenza. This was the meditation that I joined at Anne's house that brought the gate incident.

> Breaking the Habit of Being Yourself: How to Lose Your Mind and Create a New One: *feeling grateful means it has already happened*

Dispenza uses guided meditation to walk us into

imagining the life we want to live, the feelings that we want, and following this with gratitude because feeling grateful means it has already happened.

I checked out what I could visualize getting done. And then seeing what it would be like if I could feel what I wanted. And feeling gratitude for this new experience.

I was told as a kid that you don't talk about what you're going to do because you will be a loud-mouth and you won't actually do it. That formula got stuck in my mind so I couldn't talk about what I was going to do. Then I learned the scientific process of creating manifestations, and that it wasn't just mystical hodgepodge, "I'm going to say a prayer." No, there's actually a process for doing this.

Then I started looking at my ideas. I saw myself coming up with a name. I wrote about my core values as a therapist, and the type of clients I wanted but not with an agenda like, "I'm going out to get twenty clients right now." I sat with it, doing nurturing self-care, until I had more energy. Then I could do the constructive self-care of marketing, which was on my list.

I studied what I wanted to. I spent time with the kids. I did yoga. I didn't worry about getting clients. I read books. For me nurturing self-care includes play. Go swimming with the kids every day. Playing on the monkey bars.

How long had I just wanted to play? I had been stuck in "go mode" for so long that I hadn't realized how tense I was until I spent time with my kids and remembered what play felt like. They have been my play gurus.

Instead of thinking that I should be working more, I got to learn about my kids and how to be a father. It's when I wrote *Shame Free Potty Training* as I learned how to not do the common harmful things. And this was my self-care – not doing it the way I was taught or had observed. Instead being open to learning.

As I practiced avoiding getting stuck in labels, I shifted out of who I was

> *I'm just not going to do that anymore*

and what Cycle I was in. I used to change based on the people I was around, and now I'm done doing that. I'm just not going to do that anymore.

Going to College

My college experience was a great part of my evolution. I had late-night three in the morning conversations with White people all the way through college. Two people just sitting there, sometimes drinking, and they ask, "Hey, do you really worry about cops stopping you?" Or, "Have you been harassed? Has that happened to you?" I can say that, yes, I have been stopped. I have been harassed.

Then to be able to say, "And, my dad is a cop."

That blew their minds because they expected that I would hate all police because all police are bad. But I got to say how people are people and we can look at them as individuals. It's easier to take a whole group of people and say they are evil. People say, "Oh, you're Black. Oh, you're Mexican. You're this or that." But because my mother is Mexican (technically Texican) I don't fit in any category.

Those conversations were training because it taught me how to keep my cool. How to articulate. The people I talked with were ready to be vulnerable too. We could say when we were uncomfortable.

When someone says, "I don't know what your experience is and I want to know, are you willing to tell me?" they are being vulnerable. I started to see benefits. I appreciate that people actually want to be around me because they feel safe when they want to talk about things.

Calming the Amygdala

The amygdala is a portion of the brain that gets activated when we're frightened. It offers the choice between running from the source, or fighting it, or freezing in place. When calming the fear it can help to understand the functions of the autonomic nervous system. Autonomic means automatic. It is made up of two complementary systems – the sympathetic and the parasympathetic. The functions of these nerves is out of our conscious control. This includes heart functioning, organ functioning, and many other regular body events. We can't decide to increase or decrease our heart rate, but we can influence it.

The sympathetic autonomic nervous system increases the heart rate, the blood pressure, and breathing. It decreases what isn't necessary in emergencies, such as the digestive system. It heightens the fight or run response.

The parasympathetic portion does the opposite. It calms us by reducing the heart rate and blood pressure. We become more able to perceive the broad picture instead of focusing intently on emergency. You can learn more about this in *The Full Catastrophe of Living* by Jon Kabat-Zinn.

Using the Breath

The autonomic nervous system can be influenced by how you breathe. Breathing in activates the sympathetic response,

Breathing in four and breathing out eight increases calming.

increasing heart rate and blood pressure. The parasympathetic portion decreases both. So breathing in to a count of four and out for a count of eight increases the functioning of the calming portion. Tightening the throat on the outbreath with mouth open can help slow it down. You will make a soft noise.

Imagine if you see someone walking toward you and you tighten up with a fight response. What would happen if you breathed in for four, and out for eight? Enough of the irrational component might subside and allow for a more accurate evaluation. With the ability to perceive and decide, the amygdala could function more appropriately.

When I encountered the woman with the dogs, I didn't focus on the length of time I breathed in and out. I just paid attention to breathing. I did it consciously. I imagined my electromagnetic field that extends from my body expanding. And each of my seven energy centers starting with the one at my tail bone, up to the forth one at my heart. I focused on staying in the heart energy to support myself. And to project a caring person, not the frightening one I was afraid she thought I was.

You may be thinking about the obvious implication here. How is it possible to think about breath when you're frightened? Yes. Hard. So practicing breathing/meditation when we are not reactive helps conscious breathing become second nature.

The man who recorded the Karen woman verbally attacking him and calling the police was able to take care of himself. He got out his phone and made a permanent record of what she did. He must have tightened up the way I did in the park, but still was able to think about it.

I practice thinking of breathing as a way to prepare myself for frightening situations.

> *I can't yet be not afraid.*

So I was able to slow my sympathetic nerves down. This helped me think better about the situation, to see what was actually happening, not what I thought was. I can't yet be not afraid. But I have a different way of responding to the fear.

Repressed Rage

I thought that I had set aside my anger about being treated differently until reflecting on being denied entrance at the neighborhood gate. My passive numbness was a freeze response. Being able to notice the past memories of being stopped in "neighborhoods I didn't belong in," being randomly frisked going into venues (I could win the lotto for how many times I am "randomly" chosen). I continued to suppress the rage because of exhaustion from all those times where there was no resolution, just a bad taste in my mouth, and having to say, "It is what it is."

We understood that Anne had picked up my suppressed rage and acted on it. I respect her understanding of these things, and so I had to know that taking the stand of acceptance wasn't really working. Even though I had long since given up my hostile behaviors, the emotions that generated them were still there.

First I learned how to de-escalate situations. Now I have to discover what to do with rage over the discrimination against us.

You may think that the 2020 protests are taking care of it. Yes, they are changing how the world looks at racism. And they are giving us the ability to have our distress witnessed. Viral videos give us the chance to band together in anger, and also in gratitude for well-handled situations.

But every one of us carries anger that we don't know what to do with. Anger along with shame

> *We carry anger that we don't know what to do with*

passed down from our slave ancestors. Anger over horrendous treatment that continued even after the Civil War. And anger over the internalized covert racism that even caring White people exhibit.

This last is almost the worst because they think they aren't racist. They will tell you they aren't racist, "Some of my best friends are Black," "I like Black people."

My Rage
I would like to tell you that I'm not angry any more, that the way I felt at the residential gate never happens. But no. I am still learning about it.

Growing up with military relatives and with a Mexican mother, as a young child I didn't receive the racism I later encountered. I am glad to come from a military background because each person was just a person, with the focus on being American, working together to win. But even though this was good, when I found out what the rest of the world was like, it was difficult.

Dad had prepared me for profiling by police officers; how I should raise my hands and make it clear I wasn't resisting. But it was striking when I started college. My first night at Cal Poly in the small town of San Luis Obispo I was the designated driver of several friends and dorm mates who went out drinking. As we were heading back to the dorm I pulled a little to the right in order to check if it was my street as I didn't yet know my way around. As I pulled back out in the street sirens blared.

I hadn't been drinking because I had practice in the morning and didn't want to drink the night before. Everyone else in the car had been and were freaked out.

Even though my heart was racing I calmly told them I hadn't been drinking. I was the designated driver. I explained that I was an athlete and had just come to Cal Poly, and didn't know my way around yet. In other words I told them the truth in a calm manner. A manner I had learned well.

But they still had me get out of the car, walk the line and did the breathalyzer. While this occurs in most college towns, I wonder what would have happened if I reached for my wallet too fast, or if I would have argued with them as I have seen

White peers do. Would I have been allowed to leave?

Change How We Feel About Ourselves

Can you imagine Martin Luther King talking about the bus laws when Black people had to sit at the back? How Rosa Parks refused to give up her seat in front? And how the boycott was created? Did he have a victim tone: Shit, they just don't treat us right? Or did he sound firm. Ready.

All he did was name the inappropriate laws. The murders. Firmly. With passion at how it was in-

> *MLK named inappropriate laws with* self-esteem.

correct. But with *self-esteem.* What can be done about it?

I am adopting this attitude. I want to turn not to those who encourage violence, but to those who powerfully move forward non-violently.

Here's where learning how to change ourselves on the inside can influence our lives on the outside. And from there

> *Changing ourselves on the inside influences our lives on the outside*

influence the attitude toward us – first as individuals and then as a community.

When every one of us can step forward when encountering racism and say this isn't correct, the world will change. We have accessed this feeling when gathering together in demonstrations and have seen powerful changes in laws and the enforcement of laws, and also in public awareness. We have awakened so many White people that they can no longer be blind to what's going on.

Businesses are changing their practices. The media are hiring more Black people.

When we recognize our strength we create powerful change. We can combine social change with personal change on a path towards healing.

Chapter 13

Reducing Shame

Start With Reducing Shame

The shame we carry makes us feel violent and want to lash out. We want to get back at anyone who makes us feel badly about ourselves. But we are afraid to lash out so we block our feelings, and so our very humanity.

It's an internal struggle.

I saw my blocker when talking with Anne. After going into detail about writing this book, I reacted to revisiting my history, and talking about my rage. After one of our most revealing conversations I had difficulty separating my raw emotions from my acceptable ones. And I was afraid that people wouldn't be able to handle all my emotions. So I had to sift through the feelings, deciding if they were okay or not.

Even though I know this is not rational fear, I appreciate knowing that it

> *So I had to look at my shame*

comes from the three different sources of Black shame. And now I'm the one who is stuck with it. Blaming slave owners or current White supremacists doesn't help. It just fuels more rage. So I had to look at the shame. Recognize it for what it is.

When I don't feel shame, which is a wonderful respite, I can see the truth. And that is that my life is good. I know, as MLK did, that I want to continue the freeing of us from racism. When I feel competent, I get to enjoy this. I want to talk with community leaders, offering videos and information about what might help our healing process. Conversations that can help anyone get free from these massive layers of shame. I get excited when I talk with people and they want to join me in whatever we can do to move to the next level.

When I'm like this I know I'm having an impact on White people I encounter. The students in my class. Even the checkers at Trader Joe's. The friends I grew up with who I visit with regularly. My students and other college people. They turn to me with their questions, and I've become able to listen well. I discuss the issues rather than being hijacked emotionally. I say what they may need to hear to help cultivate a better understanding of what being an ally looks like.

And there are still those times when I want to attack. I have to be careful around my children. They are always there, and way too easy to harm. I tell my wife about this mood, and she gets that I need to spend time alone until I can shift back to myself.

All About Shame

Shame is the underpinning of so much that I had to address in order to improve my life. As I have said, the books that I found helpful are *Shedding Shame And Claiming Freedom: How to Eradicate Our Most Painful Emotion*, and the *Shedding Shame*

Workbook: Release the Cause of Anxiety, Depression and Lack of Self-Care, written by Anne Stirling Hastings, PhD, the Anne who has brought my words to writing. She is my colleague and even better, my friend.

Downloaded or Inherited Shame

When I first heard that we carry the anger and pain of our slave ancestors I thought this was just a way of passing the blame on to others. But it is actually true. I learned about this in my psychology training, reading the studies that reveal what is called "multigenerational trauma."

Even after growing up in a racist culture, I was shocked when hearing "Traumatic Slave Syndrome: How Is It Different From PTSD?" by Dr. Joy DeGruy Leary on YouTube. Her example is about when a White and Black mother talk, the White mother admires the gifts and abilities of the Black child, but the Black mother doesn't. This is because slave mothers denigrated their children's performance, actually denying that they are advanced.

When thinking about this, I remembered a time when I did it myself and didn't understand why. Anne mentioned that she could see some energetic gifts of my son. I know she was right because I see them too.

But when she asked me about his gifts, I only told her what he had been learning in school. I couldn't understand why I just couldn't get the words out of my mouth about his unusual abilities. Now I understand that I carry that downloaded fear of singling my children out as better than others. I didn't want to put him in danger. I irrationally feared that he would be taken away from me.

The first inherited distress I read about was the Holocaust survivors' children. They grew up and went to therapy with symptoms of being Holocaust survivors. They had taken on their parents emotions without being able to see the connection.

Anne's client who could not drive past Los Angeles International Airport (LAX) without having a panic attack had two grandparents who had been put on a train for a death camp.

Anne recognized the reason, and walked him through trauma-relieving practices. It proved helpful to understand that he was experiencing being sent to his death. Soon he was able to drive by the airport with no distress. He relieved himself of his grandparents' trauma. Knowing where the trauma originated, that it wasn't his, helped relieve the trauma response.

That's an example of downloaded fear. What about downloaded shame? Our ancestors were taught that they were worth no more than their ability to serve. To be controlled. To be raped. To live in poor housing. To be sold. To be separated from family.

While I am capable of taking care of my family, I carry genes that say I have no worth beyond serving a master.

I value understanding what got passed down to us because once I know I can change the thinking

> *I value understanding what got passed down to us*

that keeps me hardwired in a system that doesn't work towards my wellbeing. We need to see it before we can relieve ourselves of it, as the third generation Holocaust survivor did.

However, there is a big difference between Holocaust survivors and us. They were received with sympathy and compassion and seen as not deserving what happened to them. Everyone is angry at their perpetrators, considering them evil. We are united in this. What a contrast to how our country feels about slave owners.

Only now are Confederate symbols taken down. The "heroes" who were against the freedom of slaves have remained in statues, their flag revered. We are now asserting that it is right to remove all evidence of the perception of our humanity as worthy of being owned.

I was in graduate school in my early twenties when I learned about the kind of shame that was inherited from slaves. Why, I thought, did Black mothers not revel in their children's development? Why do Black parents still "whup" their kids? as addressed in the book, *Spare the Kids: Why Whupping Children Won't Save Black America*. The answer is the same. It came down from those days when beating was how slaves were forced to do what they were told.

How I Use Shame Healing

I like that the shame passed down to us can be addressed in groups. First we get to name what we feel and what we think, even what we do, as being passed along to us. It isn't who we are. We aren't defective by nature when we want to hit our kids, when we have that intense urge. When

I added shame to my feeling list it seemed monumental. I had avoided it with drugs and sex.

But once I dropped the shame of believing I was an inferior person, I could study what our ancestors had gone through.

Positive Emotions Passed Down From Pre-Slavery

I wonder how much was passed to us through our ancestors before slavery? From loving cultures. I haven't looked into this much yet, but why not? We are a loving people in addition to our anger, along with our distortions. I will explore this in my own process. Dr. DeGruy describes a trip to southern Africa to villages that haven't become Westernized and portrays some of the positives that were lost to slaves.

When writing *Shame-Free Potty Training* I was facing my tendency to get mad when my children didn't do what I wanted. Luckily I had learned from Hastings' books that shaming others comes from our own feelings of shame. The emotion of feeling badly about ourselves stops when we make someone else feel badly about themselves. My ordinary sense of shame provoked me into yelling at my kids. They hadn't done anything to trigger it except be uncontrollable. During slavery being uncontrollable always received whipping. So I was adopting the attitude of the master when my kid wouldn't do what I wanted. And what the slave parents did to make sure the children were controllable so they wouldn't be sold away or killed.

Having studied anxiety and trauma I was able to observe myself. I noticed how my heart rate increased, how I went into fight mode.

When I could see this then I could make the choice to act differently. I breathed in for the count of four, out for the count of eight knowing that this would slow my blood pressure and heart rate. I would raise my hands above my head in a style from Chi Gong that would change my overall electromagnetic energy, slowing me down, letting me be more self-aware.

If I yelled I would explain to my child that what I did was wrong. Luckily I had made enough progress when they were born that I didn't yell at them very often. But sadly, now my shame is also triggered when I have the urge to be hard on them when I operate on genetically inherited emotional reactions.

Heritage of Struggle

As a therapist I sometimes ask White clients about their heritage, how their ancestors had to struggle to become part of the White culture. And how after several generations had passed and the original cultural practices and language were gone, they "forgot" how they had signed up for a sense of belonging. But how they carried the downloaded discomfort of those who had to move to the "better" country where they believed they could have the life of their dreams.

If we see Blacks and Whites as races with basic differences we will have a hard time stopping the set-up where Black people feel like victims and White people feel like oppressors. Except for Native Americans we all came here from somewhere, and we all had to integrate. Now it's Black people's turn. And Latin American people's turn.

I learned that helping teens and adults connect with their cultural identity can cultivate emotional breakthrough that leads to further healing. They don't know about it because it isn't taught in school. We have to find out. My curiosity with slave stories let me see where I had come from. My father's knowledge of history added more.

If you think about where your ancestors came from and what they went through to become established it will make more sense of what newer Americans are going through. If you think that Black people have been here a long time, remember that we were prevented from voting until just fifty years ago. Our integration is more complex than those who immigrated together.

> *We were prevented from voting until just fifty years ago*

I find that some teens feel more confident when they can identify and connect with the struggle their ancestors had to go through. It lets them empathize with what's going on now for Black people.

One teen's parents didn't get the Black Lives Matter movement and said derogatory things about protests. They said how they should know better. They should do this, and that. This young man felt shame for trying to connect with BLM and Black people in his community.

I suggested that he bring it up, so he asked his father about when they emigrated here. When did his family first come into this country. He learned that they had emigrated from Poland during WWII. When his father talked about how they came to this country, it began a conversation about their struggle. His ancestors had immigrated through New York and then moved to the West Coast. By the time his father was a child he wasn't taught the native language. They didn't want him to have an accent. They lost contact with the family back in Poland.

They became American. By stripping away the cultural values and iden-

> *They became American*

tity the struggle was over. The teen believed that they came from money, which wasn't true. They had worked hard and become well off. This distortion caused the father to be unable to empathize. He said that Black people shouldn't feel sorry for themselves. He took things out of context in discussions.

Explaining to my client how to have a conversation in a non-reactive, nonjudgmental way allowed him to get his dad to talk. They talked about what is race, what is culture, what is ethnicity. They could talk about how their ancestors' experience was different from what is going on now. Where Black people didn't have the same resources. As slaves they hadn't even been allowed to read.

This teen felt empowered by having this conversation, and things changed. The family stopped being silent. They no longer let his grandmother make racist comments.

In college I had a roommate of Italian ancestry, and his experience was different from the teen's. He knew he was Italian. They have roots in their culture which is different from their race. They identify as "I'm White," yes, but those with an actual rooted culture are more secure when talking about it. Knowing what they come from, they have a sense of gratitude.

Most of my roommates were White but from different backgrounds. I had a Jewish roommate, a Polish roommate, and the Italian. They all had cultural connections and so were easier to talk with. Their cultural connections became stronger from our conversations because they saw the parallels with mine.

My Italian roommate had Irish ancestry too. The Italians and Irish didn't get along until they both became White. Talking about that would be powerful in schools or in families. But it's more like, "We're all White now, it's all good," versus at one time you were the outcast. The troublemakers.

When White teens get harassed by a minority group, they may find White Supremacist groups appealing. They are taught that this is your race, you are White, this is your heritage, this is your culture. If it's not explored they don't learn that no, you actually came from Poland, which was part of Nazi Germany, where your family fled from persecution.

I find it wonderful that many teenagers want the truth of what this nation is about. But if they are only taught by one angry Black person or one teacher verses the rhetoric in the family, they may feel ashamed. They may not be able to talk about it at all.

It's okay to talk about your culture. It's okay to celebrate what your ancestors had to go through to get here. We can all acknowledge that. Unless you are Native American you cannot say that this has just been your land. Your ancestors had to adjust and integrate too.

Section III

Healing Through Community

Chapter 14

Healing and Community

Groups of Us

Facing the effects of racism is difficult to do on our own. Emotional, physical, and spiritual healing of any kind is difficult to do on our own. I had several forms of community in which I could belong, or where I was able to talk about my experience as a Black person and be witnessed.

I want to include some of the ways this was possible, and invite you to discover your own. One arena open to everyone is barber shops that cater to Black men. I believe that shops for women have the same function, but not having been there I can only address those for men.

Others are setting up regular meetings with friends at homes or coffee shops. The Meetup.com organization offers many kinds of gatherings, and it is possible to create your own. Churches are a place where you may know many others, and be able to put together your own group. If it can be led by someone within the church so much the better. At work, gyms and any other place with a significant Black population you can invite two or more people to have regular conversations.

Group Invitation

My own groups have fallen together over the

years so I don't have an example for how to invite others. However, I want to offer thoughts on it.

First is in-person. If you know other Black church members, approach them one at a time. Show them a copy of this book, and ask if they would be interested in taking a look, and possibly talking about it.

Second would be writing up an invitation that you can hand out or send out. You might include an initial meeting place and time. Or you could just give contact information so they can get in touch. Include the name of the book and a paragraph or more from the intro or the back of the book, or the description in Amazon. You might start with the suggestion of a book club type of meeting rather than a full on healing together. Then after you have several readers, find out what the group of you is interested in pursuing.

If you start your own Meetup.com group you might include a discussion of covert racism and the African American system. It could include sharing examples in your lives. TruSo is Black-owned social media app and can support private and open groups for discussion and discourse.

Your group may be you and one other person, or up to five or six. This size makes room for everyone to talk. Setting an intention before the meeting or during it can help.

Figure out what you are interested in, though, because you might want a more formal group where not everyone talks, and not much processing is wanted. Then a larger group works.

Talking

My group meets at a coffee shop every week or so. We are there to delve deeply into our emotions and experiences. We are all therapists, and are used to this kind of conversation. We also relate what happens to us and what we think and feel about the subjects I have covered. It has become a lifelong process. We are committed to healing our way up the spiritual ladder to what we can accomplish in this life time.

This extensive approach isn't of course necessary. I am going over some of it for those who are interested.

Holding Council

I learned about how to hold council from this book, *The Way of Council,* by Jack Zimmerman. As I was learning how to be a therapist, I saw the

> The Way of Council, *by Jack Zimmerman shows a way to create community.*

magic of this non-therapy way of creating community that could offer safe vulnerability. Once people have that they are more likely to continue it more and more deeply.

Here is a quote from the web site, WaysofCouncil.net.

> When you find your place inside the circle, you are surrounded by a community that practices a willingness to provide you with a patient, loving, compassionate understanding of who you are, and the circle is committed to a relationship with you, and with each other, that will help you on your life's journey.

More formal than barber shops, I get a few people together with the intent of listening well to each other. And being heard. Sometimes we just take turns talking about what is important to us. Other times we have a talking stick that is passed around. Then each person knows it's their turn. Then each one also can ask for time in a non-verbal way.

I am looking at how to heal ourselves from being the objects of racism.

> *Healing from being the objects of racism*

In The Barbershop

I found that talking about my feelings of shame was the best way to extricate them from my soul. This is where my barber shop played a role. I knew that my barber would listen to what I was feeling, and not judge. He also knew to not give me advice or suggestions. I wasn't addressing much in the present, just what I projected from the past and from ancestors.

When I had fallen in love with my girlfriend, and our first child was on the way, I didn't know if I should propose marriage. I knew we were together for life. We were creating family. So why not do what people do in that situation?

But I was scared. I didn't know how much my parents' bad marriage would transfer to me. Back then I didn't know that I was also influenced by the slave experience of attaching in love and then being separated. Having children, loving them, then losing them. And partners. No control. And look at Black relationships now. Separations are common, creating single parenting for the kids.

Biracial relationships can be even more difficult because of the lack of understanding of each other's cultures and communication styles. I didn't want to live that out in my life.

My barber just asked me questions. He said "why wouldn't you want to marry her? What do you think life would be like in five years married? Single?" Open-ended questions were the key. They allowed me to explore my own fears as well as what could be. He didn't need to have an answer, he just created the space where I was allowed to feel what felt right to me, and say it out loud.

Barber Shop for Self-Care

How do we engage in a healing process so that we can let go of the irrational component of our reaction to racism? There is already a foundation in black barber shops, a place without racism. Where we go for pampering, some care taking, and where we can talk. Talk!

> *Black barber shops, without racism, are where we can talk.*

As we can focus our talk on the emotions and practices that can help us evolve, then we can even heal ourselves. When we do it together. We already have an environment in place for it.

When I was in school in San Luis Obispo I was one of the 1.2% Black people at the college and in the non-diverse town. But still there was a Black barber shop. I became so attached to my barber that when I moved down the state to Santa Barbara I drove the distance to my old barber.

As I thought about how we are able to use that setting to feel good, why not use it for healing?

My friends and I talk about it as our therapy, but after I became a therapist, I began looking at it as an actual source of therapeutic change.

In the same way that there are good therapists and bad therapists, there are wonderful barbers, and those that just want to do the job and be done with you. It's possible to check out the energy of a shop by going once and seeing how it feels. You are paying to be pampered, taken care of and made to feel good. Barbers know that you are there for more than getting your hair cleaned up. If you walk out looking forward to the next time, then you're in the right place.

I have been fortunate to find great barbers. I walk in with the mindset of being taken care of, and getting to be with Black men. No advice, just asking me questions to get me to think about it. Conversation can evolve among the other men there, too. Where else can we do that together?

I went with my grandfather when I was four. It was a rite of passage, a big deal. Being around men talking about life, talking about politics, talking about religion, talking about sports. Saying things you can say there. Talking about taboo things that you don't get to say out loud anywhere else.

I saw him engage with everyone around him, where everyone didn't have to agree with him. Where that kind of dis-

> *You may not like the dude on the corner, but he is still welcome.*

course could exist. You may not like the dude on the corner, but he is still welcome there. That's what I saw, and that's what I imitate. I want my environment to be like that. I want people to be able to talk. To know what others are thinking, and what lens they are looking through.

As a kid I got to be quiet and listen to adult men talk. In most places I feel that I have to present appropriate thoughts, and not disagree, but in the barber shop it's okay to have different views.

I got to hear preachers who came there, and professors. I listened to people from different walks of life. I get to see someone who looks like me doing something, so I can do it too. It raises the glass ceiling of what I can accomplish.

When I left for college I was on my own for a long time. There wasn't anyone in San Luis Obispo who could cut Black hair. Barbers will say that the hair's the same, but it isn't. You cut it in a different way. You have to take care of it in a different way. But it wasn't just the cut I was after.

When in college a new barber opened his shop, and I felt like I was back home. The owner became a good friend. He was great listener, and we developed a tight bond. I didn't have to make myself up. I didn't have to create an image like I did outside the barber shop where I had to look like I had it all figured out, like I had no emotions, just be cutthroat and deal with things.

> *I didn't create an image like I did outside the barber shop.*

At the barbershop I could just sit there and laugh and joke and say things I didn't have to over-explain. No accounting for why we do what we do. You don't have to explain to someone who's lived as a Black male. They get it. When I started doing self-care like meditation, and breathing, and other tools that helped, Terry would do it with me.

He began to talk with customers who were complaining about things going on in their lives, telling them to see a therapist. They would say, no that's not for me because Black people don't do therapy. We don't trust that it's okay to talk about others. When the therapist says that everything is confidential it feels like a trick.

But what is said in a barber shop isn't gossiped about. It is known that it will stay in the barber shop. We get to be us. There is safety in that.

One time when Terry had a group in the shop, he asked them what was going on. They opened up, feeling safe to share here. I pointed out how this is what happens in therapy, how feeling safe that you will be listened to and respected can help.

They got that this wasn't so bad. It wasn't the scary boogie man thing to do. When my hair cut was done in an hour or so I pointed out that this was like group therapy because there was a group of us who embraced healing, not tearing down. I asked, "Did you hear anyone laughing at you? Or criticizing you?"

Within this little world everything is normal and right. Shame free. It's like a pause for a moment.

Barber Shops Can Help Us

Barber shops are an environment where we all go, and where we can interact in helpful ways, ways that can change us for the better. It's possible to watch videos of the issues we all have, and discover ways to handle them differently. For example, breathing my way through my expectations of the White woman with the dogs can be shown right there on the video screen. Others can see how we can calm ourselves. How we can manage those situations where we have been powerless, and where we have so much anger that we lose sight of what to do.

When I don't have a barber shop I miss it. The barber may be like the therapist on the team, but the environment shapes how you feel. Your comfort and stress level.

No one has to agree, but be willing to listen, and then give their perspective. We're missing that in the world, the ability to hold space without judgment. And then people don't understand why they can't connect with others. As I grew up it was seen as normal to interact with people, and allow them to share their perspective.

Once your perspective is shared you want to invest in your listeners. And they feel invested in you.

> *"How are you doing? Really, how are you doing?"*

That's how it's always been for me. I'll talk with someone just randomly, "How are you doing? Really, how are you doing?" That's always been my grandfather.

As a therapist my attention is focused on my clients wellbeing. When a dad, a husband, and a son I take care of others.

Sitting in the Barber chair is the one time I am being taken care of. Someone is present for my wellbeing. I can drop all my other roles and just be me. Just be L.J. I can talk about my life and not have to be cautious of what I say. Or about my views. I can be 100% me. I feel recharged when I leave that chair.

Acknowledgments

Thank you to all my mentors, coaches, professors, and supporters who embraced my curiosity and encouraged me to be myself. To my friends, roommates and colleagues who I confided in and at times were my only way of grounding. To those that read the early manuscript and connected to the material. To my parents who allowed me to develop my own perspective, even if it was different than theirs. To my grandparents who invested time, and wisdom into me. Thank you to my wife and kids who have been patient with me as I worked on this project, and who continue to show so much love. Thank you Anne, for going on this journey through the up cycles and the down to get this book across the finish line.

Thank you all for not putting me in a box, for allowing me to be my authentic self. I hope this book helps you realize you are multidimensional and one box just won't fit.

About the Author

Louis J. Lumpkin is a marriage and family counselor who goes by L. J., and lives in Southern California with his wife and two children. L. J. was a track athlete at Cal Poly, then continued his education in Santa Barbara. He has worked in a variety of  addiction and mental illness recovery centers and is now in private practice. He teaches multicultural psychology and psychotherapy practicum at Pepperdine University.

L. J. gives talks internationally in person and on podcasts on the subject of healing from systemic racism. He offers training for Barbers on how to create council for those in the shop.

His next books are about parenting, and about relationships.

Books Read As a Young Person

The Souls of Black Folks, by W. E. B. Dubois.

The Norton Anthology of African American Literature, by Henry Louis Gates, Jr., Valerie Smith, et al.

Narrative of the Life of Frederick Douglass, by Frederick Douglass.

Twelve Years a Slave, by Solomon Northup.

References

The Full Catastrophe of Living, by Jon Kabat-Zinn.

The Art of Living: Peace and Freedom in the Here and Now, by Thich Nhat Hahn.

Breaking the Habit of Being Yourself: How to Lose Your Mind and Create a New One, by Dr. Joe Dispenza.

Shedding Shame and Claiming Freedom: How to Eradicate Our Most Painful Emotion, by Anne Stirling Hastings, PhD.

Shedding Shame Workbook: Release The Cause of Depression, Anxiety, and Lack of Self Care, by Anne Stirling Hastings, PhD.

Post Traumatic Slave Syndrome: America's Legacy of Enduring Injury and Healing, by Joy A. Degruy.

Shame-Free Potty Training: A New Approach for A New Generation, by Louis J. Lumpkin III, Anne Stirling Hastings.

The Wisdom of Cells, by Bruce Lypton.

The Biology of Belief, by Bruce Lypton.

The Body Keeps the Score: Brain: Mind and Body in the Healing of Trauma, by Bessel van der Kolk.

Spare the Kids: Why Whupping Children Won't Save Black America, by Stacey Patton

The Genogram Journey, by Monica McGoldrick.

The Way of Council, by Jack Zimmerman.

TruSo is a Black-owned social media app.

Made in the USA
Las Vegas, NV
28 February 2022